visions of Mary

by Barbara Calamari & Sandra DiPasqua

Abrams, New York

Editor: Christopher Sweet
Editorial Assistant: Sigi Nacson
Designer: Sandra DiPasqua
Production Manager: Maria Pia Gramaglia

Library of Congress Cataloging-in-Publication Data
Calamari, Barbara.
 Visions of Mary / Barbara Calamari & Sandra DiPasqua.
     p. cm.
 Includes bibliographical references and index.
 ISBN 978-0-8109-5581-3 (hardcover)
 1. Mary, Blessed Virgin, Saint. I. DiPasqua, Sandra. II. Title.

BT603.C35 2004
232.91—dc22
                                    2004008765

10 9 8 7 6 5 4 3 2

harry n. abrams, inc.
a subsidiary of La Martinière Groupe
115 West 18th Street
New York, NY 10011
www.hnabooks.com

acknowledgements

This was a complicated project and we were lucky to have the help and enthusiasm of so many different people. At Abrams we have a wonderful working relationship with our editor Christopher Sweet and his assistant Sigi Nacson. Our agent Jim Fitzgerald has always been generous with his ideas and support for our projects. The Marian Library at the University of Dayton has been a major source for those doing research on the Virgin Mary since 1943. Not only did we use this library to check facts and information, but Father Thomas Thompson has been a great and generous help in researching pictures and allowing us the use of their images. Deborah Rust and Brian Tully provided us with much needed technical help, and Dan Wilby was invaluable in photographing our delicate printed holy cards. Patricia Bates and Louis Turchioe are owed a special thanks for their constant support over the years.

We wanted *Visions of Mary* to be a book about how the Virgin Mary affects people in their everyday lives. In some countries and in many homes and businesses in the United States, images of Mary are displayed among other family photographs. For this reason, we deliberately chose not to use the great art works and paintings that have been created in her honor. Rather, we sought photographs of "everyday Marys.". We were extremely fortunate to relate our ideas to the photographer Lisa Silvestri before she took a trip to Mexico, Cuba, and New Orleans. She returned with countless beautiful images which helped us set the visual tone of our book. Our only regret is that we did not have room for more of her work. Lisa's color photographs were printed by Hong Digital, New York City and her black and white photographs printed by 68 Degrees, New York City. Dr. Joseph Sciorra of the Calandra Center in New York City was not only generous in sharing his research on the black Madonnas of Southern Italy, but he introduced us to the work of two terrific photographers, Larry Raccioppo of New York City and Dana Salvo of Gloucester, Massachusetts. Diane Block, photo archivist at The Museum of New Mexico, deserves thanks for her help in finding photographs for this book.

Father Eugene Carrella provided us with several beautiful holy cards from his extensive collection. Through his insistence we made the acquaintance of Micki Cesario and her husband Michael. Micki has a major holy card collection devoted to depictions of the Virgin Mary from all over the world. Her patience and generosity in allowing us to use these images has graced this book with much beauty. It is our hope that we have done her collection the justice it deserves.

Finally we are indebted to the shrine of Akita, Japan, for allowing us to use the image of their statue and to the Zeitun Coptic Outreach Center and the Monastery of Saint Mina for their permission in using the Egyptian-television images of the apparitions at Zeitoun.

This book is dedicated to the memory of Karen Dottling.

contents

A little girl's altar made by her grandmother,
Mexico City, Mexico.

"Do whatever He tells you."

The Roman Catholic love and respect for the Virgin Mary divides it from other sects of Christianity. Mary is not only revered as the Mother of God but also as the Mother of all Humanity, and her image continually watches over every aspect in the daily life of Catholic countries. She is credited with working miracles through pictures, statues, and sacred earthly places. She is the inspiration of much of the world's greatest music, art, and architectural works. Her spiritual gifts are recognized in the East and both Hindus and Buddhists refer to her as Mother Mary. Muslims revere her as the mother of a great prophet and she is the only woman with her own chapter in the Koran. As a human being Mary is able to relate directly to the major and minor sufferings of mankind. For this reason she is not prayed to as a goddess, but rather, called on by Catholics to aid them in their prayers. It is thought that she shares her constant flow of grace with those who ask, bringing them closer to God. Thomas Merton wrote, "Mary does not rule us from without, but from within. She does not change us by changing the world around us, but she changes the world around us by first changing our own inner lives."

In chapter 2 of John's Gospel is the story of the Wedding at Cana: On the third day there was a wedding in Cana in Galilee, and the mother of Jesus was there. Jesus and his disciples were also invited to the wedding. When the wine ran short, the mother of Jesus said to him, "They have no wine." Jesus said to her, "Woman, how does your concern affect me? My hour has not yet come." His mother said to the servers, "Do whatever he tells you." Now there were six stone water jars there for Jewish ceremonial washings, each holding twenty to thirty gallons. Jesus told them, "Fill the jars with water." So they filled them to the brim. Then he told them, "Draw some out now and take it to the headwaiter." So they took it. And when the headwaiter tasted the water that had become wine, without knowing where it came from (although the servers who had drawn the water knew), the headwaiter called the bridegroom and said to him, "Everyone serves good wine first, and then when people have drunk freely, an inferior one; but you have kept the good wine until now." Jesus did this as the beginning of his signs in Cana in Galilee and so revealed his glory, and his disciples began to believe in him.

It was at His mother's request that Jesus performed His first great miracle. To Him, as a divine spiritual being, running out of wine at a wedding was no great shame. Mary, being human, realized how embarrassing such an event could be for the bride and groom. Because He so respected His mother, Jesus changed the water at the wedding into wine. As a result of this act, His disciples

introduction

became true believers. The story of the wedding at Cana is frequently cited to illustrate why Catholics have such fervent love for the Virgin Mary. It is also proof of her place in God's divine plan for mankind. Through her prodding, the first miracle of Christ was performed and because of this first miracle, those who might have doubted Christ's teachings became believers.

For Catholics, Mary sets an example of a human being who accepts all that God wills without questioning. When Mary was a young girl, the Archangel Gabriel came to her with the announcement, "Hail Mary, full of grace…" Though she was a virgin, she accepted and gave her consent to the Incarnation of Christ. For this reason she is considered one who collaborates with the work of God. Because she is the mother of Christ and He is part of the Holy Trinity, she is given the title Theotokos or "Mother of God." It is believed that Mary had full knowledge of the terrible fate that awaited her Son on Earth. Yet she also had the faith to withstand His torments because she knew that He would never die. After His Ascension into heaven, she worked with the Apostles, serving as the highest example of an advanced spiritual being who lived by Christ's teachings while on Earth. Because of this, Catholics believe that she herself did not die, but was assumed into heaven. The first sighting of Mary after her Assumption occurred in Puy, France in A.D. 47. She has been appearing to humanity ever since, offering unconditional love, healing, moral support, and in the last two centuries, warnings over the fate of mankind.

On the site of what is now Chartres Cathedral in France, the druids had a shrine devoted to the "Virgin who gives birth" one hundred years before Christ. The coming of Mary was predicted by the prophet Elijah, who led a small community devoted to her on what is now Mount Carmel in Israel eight hundred years before her birth. The oldest proved artistic images of Mary were wall paintings done in the Catacombs of Rome in the late first century. Pagans who were accustomed to worshipping both male and female deities felt comfortable with images of Mary. They related her to the earth and to their own mothers. Statues and paintings of her holding the Christ child illustrated the basic bond between Christ and humanity, and served to bring many into the Christian fold. By the Middle Ages, a time when art, religious worship, and daily life were completely harmonious, the cult of Mary was a mainstay of both the Roman and Orthodox Churches. The mystical writer and doctor of the Churches, Saint Bernard of Clairvaux insisted in the power of Mary's grace. He saw her as the messenger of original spiritual values and the ultimate mediator, always pleading the cause of the

PRECEDING PAGE: Memorial wall, East New York, New York.
OPPOSITE: Home altar in Havana, Cuba.

human race. Catholic art, which is believed to be inspired by the Holy Spirit, abounded with images of her, and the world's greatest cathedrals were erected in her honor. When the founders of the Reformation sought to stem the tide of Papal excess by bringing Christian worship back to its biblical roots, Mary's role in Christian worship was reassessed. Since there are few mentions of Mary in the Bible, reverence for her as a heavenly mediator was looked upon as superstition. She was considered to be a holy woman, long dead and buried. Visual art was considered a distraction to spiritual worship and images of Mary were considered idolatrous; many of the great Marian shrines of Germany and England were summarily destroyed. Because of this, the Virgin Mary became an important symbol of the Counter-Reformation. To Catholics, her denigration by the newly formed Protestant sects was equal to the denigration of her Son. The belief in her place as the most exalted human was expounded with a new force. Religious orders such as the Jesuits and the Carmelites spread devotions centered around the gifts of the rosary to Saint Dominic and the scapular to Saint Simon Stock. The baroque art movement was embraced in Catholic countries as a fervid symbol of their belief in art as a religiousexperience and as a direct reaction against the perceived dourness of Protestant churches. As visual representations of the Virgin Mary became more dramatic, so did stories of her rescuing or advising humanity. Most of these tales center on Mary acting through statues, paintings, or dreams.

The cult of Mary has remained strong in the Mediterranean and in Latin America. These are places where women traditionally hold the family together. Popular depictions of Mary vary from country to country and she seems to adapt the persona of the culture in which she appears. Italy and Latin America welcome the sweeter, long suffering, human, and maternal Mary. In France the Virgin Mary takes on a more ethereal and graceful persona. Spain, Portugal, and eastern Europe all have apparitions made by Mary that are more stern and serious.

It is said that the modern age of Mary was ushered in with the visits paid to Saint Catherine Laboure in 1831. Since then, the Blessed Mother has been seen steadily by seers in almost every country in the world. In this book we relate some of the Marian apparitions that are sanctioned by the Catholic Church; there are thousands more that are well known but unofficial. When Mary visits, she appears in the race of and speaking the language of the person who sees her. She can be sweet and kind or angry and insistent. The visionaries who see her enjoy no great material reward. They are often people who have little religious belief. They are usually mocked and harassed by their own community. Many have died young, not having been spared by the parameters of the lives they were born into. Some are honored in their lifetime, some choose to retire from the world, others continue on with their lives, never again experiencing any supernatural or spiritual events. The messages they relay from Mary for the human race are all basically the same, *"Do whatever He tells you."*

Home altar in Mexico City, Mexico.

titles of Mary

adam's deliverance **advocate of eve** advocate of sinners **all chaste all fair and immaculate** all good annunciation of the blessed virgin **aqueduct of grace** archetype to purity and innocence **ark gilded by the holy spirit** ark of the covenant **assumption of the blessed virgin** basilica of saint mary major **blessed among women** blessed mother **blessed virgin mary** bridal chamber of the lord **bride of christ** bride of heaven **bride of the canticle** bride of the father **bride unbrided** cause of our joy **chosen before the ages** comfort of christians **comforter of the afflicted** conceived without original sin **consoler of the afflicted** co-redemptrix **court of the eternal king** created temple of the creator **crown of virginity** daughter of men **david's daughter** deliverer from all wrath **deliverer of christian nations** destroyer of heresies **dispenser of grace** dwelling place for god **dwelling place of the illimitable** dwelling place of the spirit **earth unsown earth untouched and virginal** eastern gate ever green and fruitful ever virgin **eve's tears redeeming** exalted above the angels **feast of the immaculate conception** fleece of heavenly rain **flower of jesse's root** formed without sin **forthbringer of god** forthbringer of the ancient days **forthbringer of the tree of life** fountain of living water **fountain sealed from every stain** full of grace **garden enclosed** gate of heaven **god's eden** god's olive tree **god's vessel** handmaid of the lord **healing balm of integrity** health of the sick **helper of all in danger** holy in soul and body **holy mountain of our lord** hope of christians **house built by wisdom** house of gold **immaculate conception** immaculate heart **immaculate heart of mary** inviolate **joseph's spouse** kingly throne **king's mother** lady most chaste **lady most venerable** lady of good help **lady of grace** lady of mercy **lady of peace** lady of perpetual help **lady of the rosary** lady of sorrows **lady of victory** lamp unquenchable **life-giver to posterity** light cloud of heavenly rain **lily among thorns** living temple of the deity **loom of the incarnation** madonna **madonna of saint luke** marketplace for salutary exchange **mary of the hurons** mary the blessed virgin **mary help of christians** mary mother of god **mary queen of africa** mary queen of angels **mary queen of peace** mary star of the sea **mediatrix** mediatrix and conciliatrix **mediatrix of all graces** mediatrix of salvation **mediatrix of the mediator** minister of life **mirror of justice** more beautiful than beauty **more glorious than paradise** more gracious than grace **more holy than the cherubim the seraphim and the entire angelic hosts** morning star **most venerable mother and virgin mother** most admirable mother **most amiable mother** most chaste mother **most pure mother** inviolate mother of christians **mother of divine grace** mother of god **mother of good counsel** mother of jesus christ **mother of men** mother of our creator **mother of our head mother of our savior** **mother of the church mother of the mystical body mother of wisdom** mother undefiled **my body's healing my soul's saving** mystical rose **nativity of the blessed virgin** nature's re-creation **nature's restoration** neck of the mystical body **never fading wood** new eve **notre dame cathedral of paris** notre dame of chartres **notre dame of easton** nourisher of god and man **olive tree of the father's compassion** only bridge of god to men **our immaculate queen** our lady gate of heaven **our lady help of christians** our lady mother of the church **our lady**

La Santissima Vergine della Consolata
DI TORINO.

GOSPA OD MILOSRDJA
Kapucini - Dubrovnik

Propriété 1906.   C. van de Vyvere-Petyt, Bruges.
Notre Dame du Congo,
vénérée dans l'Eglise des Pères Rédemptoristes à Matadi.

Notre-Dame du Bon Conseil

115   Pd. in Switzerland

LE MARIAGE DE LA T.S.VIERGE ET DE S.JOSEPH
O Marie et Joseph, protégez les familles chrétiennes
et enrichissez-les de vos vertus !

Nach mein lieben Gott ergeben,
O Maria, Mutter mein,
Laß mich tragen ohne Klagen
Und wie Du geduldig sein!

PATRONAGE OF MOTHER OF GOD

MADONNA DEL ROSARIO

Madonna di Loreto

MARIA SANTISSIMA DELLA CATENA

MOTHER OF DIVINE GRACE

NOSTRA SIGNORA DEL CENAGOLO

DEPOSÉ

22

キリストの母

No.75　　　　　Mater Christi　　　　Curmel Tokyo

AVE COR PURISSIMUM
SPIRITUS SANCTI
HABITACULUM!

O.L.V. van Rust te Heppeneert bij Maeseijck.
Steendruk Karel van de Vyvere Petyt. Brugge.

Notre Dame de la Treille
patronne de Lille

Receive my beloved son, this habit of thy order: this shall be to thee and to all Carmelites a privilege, that whosoever dies clothed in this shall never suffer eternal fire.... It shall be a sign of salvation, a protection in danger, and a pledge of peace.

Our Lady of Mount Carmel

Mount Carmel, in what is today northern Israel, has always been a place rich in mystical tradition. The word *hakkarmel* means "the garden" in Hebrew, and true to its title, there is a remarkable profusion of plants and wildflowers on this mountain. It is considered a natural paradise and a sacred place, and in biblical times it was forbidden to disturb any of the natural life on it. Those who wanted to ascend the mountain for meditation lived in caves so as not to intrude on the landscape with unnatural structures.

In about 860 B.C., the prophet Elijah (also known as Elias) arrived on this holy mountain to begin a life of contemplation and prayer. The First Book of Kings is filled with tales of wonders he performed and prophesies he gave. In his prophetic visions on Mount Carmel, Elijah became aware of the coming of the mother of the Messiah. He and his followers mystically dedicated themselves to her, setting an example as the first monks. The descendants of these ancient contemplatives were among the first to accept the teachings of Christ and to be baptized by His apostles. Upon meeting Mary after Christ's Ascension, they were so overcome by her sanctity that they returned to the mountain to build a chapel in her honor. For the next thousand years Mount Carmel continued to be a place where hermits devoted themselves to prayer.

B. V. DEL CARMINE

By the twelfth century, pilgrims from Europe who had followed the Crusades to the Holy Land settled with the ascetics on Carmel and started a religious holy order known as Brothers of the Blessed Virgin Mary of Mount Carmel. Their rule, which was given in 1209 by the Patriarch of Jerusalem, says that all converges toward the contemplation of God. The *Rule of Mysticism* exhorts those who follow it to live a life of continual prayer, obedience to a superior, perpetual abstinence and fasting, manual work, and total silence.

This gift from Mary helped the Carmelites explain the historical significance of their order to the laypeople; it served as a reminder that belief in Mary as the Mother of God extended back to the Old Testament with the prophet Elijah. After Pope John XXII (r. 1316–1334) had a vision of Mary where she promised those wearing the brown scapular, "I, the Mother of Grace, shall descend on the Saturday after their death and whomsoever I find in Purgatory, I shall free, so that I may lead them to the holy mountain of everlasting life," the scapular became extremely popular among the common people. By the end of the sixteenth century it had become smaller in size and very similar to the one that is worn today. Admiration for the Carmelite Order spread as their adherence to the rules of solitude and prayer produced some of the greatest mystical saints in Catholicism, all of whom had visions of or openhearted communications with Mary. Among them are Saint Simon Stock, Saint Teresa, Saint John of the Cross, and Saint Thérèse of Lisieux.

Though the original scapular handed to Saint Simon Stock was brown wool cloth without a picture, the Carmelite scapular that is now worn and the one that is most favored now has an image of Our Lady of Mount Carmel holding the Baby Jesus while she offers the scapular. The other piece of cloth often has a picture of Jesus as a man. Neither image is prescribed. Wearing the scapular is a form of prayer and is considered a visible sign of consecrating oneself to Mary and to accepting her maternal protection.

Devotion to Our Lady of Carmel can be found wherever the Carmelites founded a monastery or convent. Many small towns in Italy have churches named after this aspect of Mary. As the townspeople emigrated to other countries, they brought the devotion with them. In many cities in the United States these churches have great celebrations in honor of Our Lady of Mount Carmel.

Artistic representations of Our Lady of Mount Carmel depict her either appearing in the sky over Mount Carmel itself or holding Jesus as a toddler. In both versions the figure of Mary is often depicted offering the scapular to the viewer. Tradition has it that the prophet Elijah saw Mary appear in the clouds over Mount Carmel eight hundred years before her birth. Sometimes this representation includes her handing the scapular to Saint Simon Stock. The other version of this aspect of Mary illustrates the Sabbatine privilege where Mary vows to take the souls of those who died wearing the brown scapular out of purgatory on the Saturday after their death. Purgatory is depicted in flames because it is a place where the soul goes to have its sins burned away.

Hail Mary, Full of Grace! the Lord is with you; Blessed are you among women, and blessed is the fruit of your womb Jesus. Holy Mary, Mother of God, pray for us sinners, now and at the hour of our death. Amen.

Altar in family mausoleum in Havana, Cuba.

I am the compassionate mother of you and your people here in this land and all of the other people who love me, call to me, search for me, and confide in me. I will listen to their pain, suffering, and crying and heal them from their misery.

Our Lady of Guadalupe

A traveler visiting Mexico or the American Southwest meets Our Lady of Guadalupe hundreds of times a day. Her image adorns the walls of businesses, is prominently displayed in homes, is on the hubcaps of cars, and at the center of small sidewalk shrines. This image of Mary is the preeminent cultural icon for most Latin Americans, sacred to Catholics and highly honored by non-Catholics, and it is the only apparition of Mary sanctioned by the Church on the North American continent.

On December 9, 1531, an Aztec convert to Catholicism named Juan Diego was on his way to early morning Mass in the area that is now known as Mexico City when he heard the sound of birds singing. When they quieted down, the hill at Tepeyac seemed to respond to their song. From the top of the hill a woman gently called to Diego, "Ihuantzin. Ihuan Diegotzin." She was speaking the Aztec language of Nahuatl. As he approached her, he saw that she was an Indian noblewoman. He was amazed at how her clothes glimmered like the sun and how the rocks and foliage around her had a heightened glow. The crag where her foot rested gave off rays of light and the earth sparkled like a rainbow.

She spoke to him courteously and with great charm, "Know my dearest, littlest, and youngest son, I am the forever whole and perfect maiden Saint Mary, honorable mother of the true God, honorable mother of the giver of life, honorable mother of the creator of men and women, honorable mother of the one who is far and close, honorable mother of the one who makes the heavens and the earth. My wish is for them to build my temple here where I will give people all my love, compassion, assistance, and protection. I am the compassionate mother of you and your people here in this land and all of the other people who love me, call to me, search for me, and confide in me. I will listen to their pain, suffering, and crying and heal them from their misery."

She then sent him to see the bishop to make the request for the church. After a long wait he related his story to the bishop who told him that he must obtain a sign proving that this was truly an appearance of Mary. Juan Diego returned to the woman on the hill and begged her to get someone more prestigious to give her message to the bishop. She told him that she had many people who could deliver her request, "but it is of precise detail that you yourself solicit and assist and that through your mediation my wish be complied."

On his next visit to the bishop he was once again greeted with suspicion. When he left, the bishop sent servants to spy on him and to see to whom he was really speaking. But as soon as Juan Diego crossed the wooden bridge to the hill at Tepeyac, they lost sight of him. The next day, a Monday, Juan Diego decided to take another route around the hill in order to avoid the woman. His uncle had taken ill, and he needed medical attention. Juan Diego did not want the woman to detain him, as he feared that his uncle would die waiting for help. Much to his dismay, she came down the hill to meet him from where she was watching. When she asked him why he was so upset and why he was in such a rush, he sadly told her about his uncle's illness and how his requests for her to the bishop had fallen on deaf ears.

Her answer was, "Listen, put it into your heart, youngest and dearest son, nothing should scare or concern you. Don't worry. Don't be afraid of the sickness, or any other illness or hardship. Am I not right here who is your mother? Are you not under my shadow and protection? Am I not in the foundation of your being, your sustenance, your happiness, peace, and effortlessness? Are you not in the fold of my garment? Do you need anything else? Don't allow anything to worry or disturb you anymore. Don't worry about your uncle's illness. He will not die. Be assured, he is already well."

She then told Juan Diego to gather roses among the rocks. He was surprised to find them in full bloom since it was winter. She carefully arranged them in Juan Diego's cloak and he brought them to the bishop. After another humiliating wait, he was finally granted an audience. As he unwrapped his cloak and the roses fell out, the bishop gasped. The flowers uncovered an elaborate portrait of the Virgin Mary imprinted on the cloak. The bishop fell to his knees in tears and begged Juan Diego's forgiveness. The

Outdoor shrine in the San Angel colonial section of Mexico City, Mexico.

bishop then insisted on being taken to the hill where the lady from heaven wanted her temple. After he had done this, Juan Diego ran home to his sick uncle and was quite shocked to see him happy and healthy. His uncle told him that a heavenly lady had come to heal him, asking him to tell the bishop of his cure. She also wanted him to convey the proper name for her image: The Perfect Virgin Holy Mary of Guadalupe.

The bishop had the church built and the cloth put on public display where it immediately attracted crowds of pilgrims. Almost as suddenly, the Franciscans, who had been in Mexico for the past ten years and who had very little previous success, were receiving thousands of Aztecs who wanted to convert to Catholicism. This cloth and its image, which should have deteriorated in twenty years, is still on view at the Basilica of Our Lady of Guadalupe in Mexico City. After almost five hundred years it remains in pristine condition. Attracting more than ten million pilgrims a year, Our Lady of Guadalupe is the most popular Marian shrine in the world.

At the time of this apparition of Mary, the Aztecs, the original inhabitants of Mexico City, had been suffering brutally under domination of the Spanish colonialists. Disease and depression were rampant. Hernán Cortés, the conquistador, had landed in 1519 and had succeeded in destroying much of the Aztec civilization by 1521. Why, then, were the Aztecs eventually such willing converts to Catholicism? The Aztecs had hundreds of gods in their pantheon. It was their spiritual habit to co-opt the gods of tribes that they conquered. They believed that their own god Huitzilopochtli depended on human sacrifices to be kept alive. They invaded neighboring tribes to obtain these victims. As they as a people became more aggressive against their neighbors, the gods of the Aztecs took on more monstrous forms. Portrayals of the female gods became the most frightening and grotesque. When the Spanish arrived in the Aztec city, they were amazed at its beauty and grace, and equally horrified at the blood-soaked temples with the racks of human skulls and demonic-looking statuary. All Aztec places of worship were considered satanic and systematically destroyed.

The hill where Mary appeared was once the site of the goddess Tonzantin. She was considered a household god, the goddess of corn and fertility. With Our Lady of Guadalupe, the feminine traits of love, compassion, and forgiveness were returned to spirituality and the sick-at-heart population had an entity to whom they could take their sorrow.

Statue of Blessed Juan Diego wearing the tilma with the imprint of Our Lady of Guadalupe.
FOLLOWING PAGES: Statues being sold at a flea market, an outdoor shrine with Our Lady of Guadalupe surrounded by lights so that she can be worshiped at night.

The portrait of Our Lady of Guadalupe conveyed a message interpreted differently by Aztecs and Europeans, yet triggered the same spiritual response. To the Aztecs, the basic announcement that Mary was making with this image was the dawning of the age of the Sixth Sun. Dividing up their history into solar ages, it was thought that the Fifth Sun, the Sun of Movement, ended with the Spanish conquest. Since the birth of a new sun always follows a time of darkness, it was believed that the appearance of Mary after ten years of destruction signaled the beginning of the Sun of Flowers. According to their lore, this was a time when humanity would come into its own and bloom. In this image, Mary wears a belt worn by pregnant women, thus announcing the birth of a new age. Gold-leaf Nahuatl glyphs symbolizing plenitude appear on her gown. They are arranged over her womb in a pattern that represented the four points of a compass, a basic symbol in the Aztec faith. The womblike light she is wrapped in, the rays of the sun and the crest of the moon, the folds of her robe and the subdued serpent all had hidden messages that were easy for the Aztecs to read. Her eyes do not stare ahead as depictions of the gods do; rather she is looking down at humanity, much as a mother looks at her child. Her hands are in a praying position that the Aztecs used to signify something coming from one's heart. The fact that her robe is touching the angel signifies protection and love.

For the Christians the iconography of this image was directly related to the book of Revelation where John says, "A great sign appeared in the heavens, a woman clothed with the sun." This image is associated with the Immaculate Conception. December 9, the first day of her appearance, was also the original day devoted to the Feast of the Immaculate Conception. The halo Mary is wrapped in is called a *mandorla*. Originally, this type of almond-shaped body halo represented the cloud in which Christ ascended; in time it came to signify the light that emanates from those divinely inspired. In Western art it is used to depict those with a complete bond to Christ. As the Mother of God, Mary is exalted above all angels, offering her protection and love to humanity.

By appearing as a mixed-race woman, Mary was announcing the new face of Catholicism. The brutal, fundamentalist way that Catholicism was practiced by the Spanish was softened. In her appearance Mary was reminding the Europeans that they had the same mother that the Aztecs did. She was the first Christian image that the Mesoamericans could relate to, and the messages embedded in her picture offered hope, love, and comfort to a people when these qualities had been driven out of their own religion.

OUR LADY OF GUADALUPE IS THE PATRONESS OF MEXICO, NORTH AND SOUTH AMERICA, AND THE CARIBBEAN. **The Feast of Our Lady of Guadalupe is December 12, the day the miraculous cloth was revealed.**

Personalized art from the flea market in Mexico City, Mexico.

In 1954, when the writer Ernest Hemingway won the Nobel Prize for his novella *The Old Man and the Sea*, he wanted to give the medal to the Cuban people. The best way he could think to accomplish this was to bring the prize to the Sanctuary of Our Lady of Cobre and dedicate it to her.

Our Lady of Cobre

Our Lady of Cobre is considered the mother of Cuban people regardless of their race, political allegiance, or ideology. She is so entrenched in the Cuban national identity that she is virtually the only unifying force between those in exile and those who remained on the island. Though Cuba has been officially declared an atheist country by its government, it allowed four Catholic masses to be said at the major cathedrals in honor of Our Lady of Cobre to commemorate a papal visit in January 1998. The first masses that took place in the middle of the country drew a respectful but reticent response. By the time the fourth mass was said in Havana, the sight of millions of joyful, chanting devotees singing and dancing in the streets so shocked the ruling powers that they agreed to loosen the laws suppressing religious feasts and celebrations in all houses of worship. To many it was proof that the Virgin Mary is far more powerful than any government.

The story of Our Lady of Cobre took place in 1606. Two brothers of Indian lineage, Rodrigo and Juan de Hoyos, and a ten-year-old African slave

Yo Soy
La Virgen de la Caridad

named Juan Moreno took a canoe out off the coast of Santiago del Prado. This was an area newly rich in copper mines, the name of which has since been changed to Cobre, *cobre* being the Spanish word for "copper." The boys were out to gather salt to preserve meat for the copper miners. Halfway across the Bay of Nipe they had to encamp on an islet because a violent storm had blown up. They waited through a harrowing night, the storm ending at daybreak. When the sea calmed the boys again set out on their task.

Almost immediately they saw a white bundle on a plank floating on the waves, approaching them. At first they thought it was a seabird, but as it neared them it appeared to be a little girl. Gradually they realized it was a statue of the Virgin Mary holding the Christ child. Much to their amazement the statue was completely dry. Inscribed on the plank were the words: "Yo soy la Virgen de la Caridad" (I am the Virgin of Charity).

The boys carried the statue back to the town, where its arrival was recognized as a message from the Virgin Mary. A shrine was constructed, and it immediately became a pilgrimage site. The statue is now in its own

OUR LADY OF COBRE IS THE PATRONESS OF CUBA. **Her feast day is September 8.**

A Botanica in
Brooklyn, New York.

sanctuary known as Nuestra Senora del la Caridad de Cobre Basilica in
Santiago de Cuba.

The statue of Our Lady of Cobre is about sixteen inches high. Artistic
depictions of it vary. The statue in the basilica is a mixed-race Mary. Though
her original robes were white, she now wears heavily brocaded golden robes
with gold and silver embroidery containing Cuba's national shield. The
stiffness of this fabric gives the statue its triangular shape. Our Lady of
Charity is a common figure found in Spanish hospitals, and it was thought
that this statue could have originally come from a Spanish ship headed for

Cuba. In later retellings of the story, the three men in the boat became the "three Juans," one European, one Taino Indian, and the third one African, who, caught out in a storm, prayed to the Virgin to save them. Miraculously, the sea calmed and the little statue floated to them out of nowhere. In art they are shown rowing in a rough sea with Our Lady of Cobre hovering over them in a protective way. In this depiction of Mary she is holding up the Baby Jesus, and both He and Mary wear golden crowns. She is standing on a half-moon, but unlike the statues of Our Lady of Charity in Spain, the moon is pointing downward. This is thought to be a particular message to the Taino Indians. Their goddess Guabonito had the symbol of the rainbow to represent her. It is thought that in this statue Mary is standing on what could be interpreted as the moon by Europeans and Africans and as a rainbow by the Tainos, offering the same gift of healing that the rainbow symbolizes to them. In art, Mary is frequently depicted as light-skinned and wearing the colors of the Cuban flag. To the island's practitioners of Santeria, Our Lady of Cobre holds an exalted position in their pantheon as the goddess Ochun. She is the goddess of love, money, and household happiness.

Throughout the nineteenth century, Our Lady of Cobre became a Cuban symbol of unity in their desire for independence from Spain. In 1916 she was named the official patroness of Cuba after soldiers who credited her intervention for their liberation from Spain petitioned the Vatican. She has always remained a symbol of the Cuban people. In 1954 when the writer Ernest Hemingway won the Nobel Prize for his novella *The Old Man and the Sea*, he wanted to give the medal to the Cuban people. The best way he could think to accomplish this was to bring the prize to the Sanctuary of Our Lady of Cobre and dedicate it to her. There it remains to this day. Wherever Cubans are in the world, her feast day is a major celebration for them. Our Lady of Cobre is fondly called by the nickname Cachita. She is a much loved member of Cuban families and her image is the one consistent thing found among exiles fleeing the island and those who live in Cuba. She is the symbol both of faith and of national identity.

Hail Mary Full of Grace! the Lord is with you; Blessed are you among women, and blessed is the fruit of your womb Jesus. Holy Mary, Mother of God, pray for us sinners, now and at the hour of our death. Amen.

CARITATIS IN FLUCTIBUS MARIS

MATER   AMBULAVIT

Andrew Jackson himself insisted that the victory was a "signal interposition of heaven." In gratitude he went out of his way to visit the Ursuline nuns at their convent and thank them for their prayer, "Our Lady of Prompt Succor, Hasten to help us!"

Our Lady of Prompt Succor

Our Lady of Prompt Succor is the name of a statue created about two hundred years ago as the result of a nun's answered prayers. Devotion to the Virgin Mary under this title is extremely strong in the city of New Orleans, where the statue's shrine is. She is invoked for a quick and favorable response by all those in need, and it is common practice for her devotees to recite the prayer, "Our Lady of Prompt Succor, Hasten to help us!" for protection against hurricanes, which frequently threaten that part of the United States.

The French Ursuline nuns, a religious order devoted to the education of young girls, first arrived in New Orleans in 1727. They created several schools with the help of nuns from Spain. In 1800 Louisiana reverted back to French control, and the Spanish nuns fled, fearing the anticlericalism of the French government. Severely lacking in staff, the Mother Superior wrote to her cousin in France for more nuns to join them. At that time, the French government made life for the religious orders extremely difficult. Mother Saint Michel Gensoul, the recipient of the letter, was discouraged by her bishop from leaving France. The order was shorthanded, and he felt he could not afford to lose any teachers to the New World. He gave her permission to write to the pope to formally request this transfer and agreed to abide by whatever decision she received. Because he was then a prisoner of Napoléon, it seemed unlikely that the pope would even see her letter, much less grant her request.

**OUR LADY OF PROMPT SUCCOR
HASTEN TO HELP US!**
MIRACULOUS STATUE OF OUR LADY OF PROMPT SUCCOR
VENERATED AT THE NATIONAL VOTIVE SHRINE
2635 STATE STREET, NEW ORLEANS, LOUISIANA

As she sent her letter, Mother Saint Michel prayed to the Virgin, "O most Holy Virgin Mary, if you obtain for me a prompt and favorable answer to this letter, I promise to have you honored at New Orleans under the title of Our Lady of Prompt Succor."

Much to everyone's amazement, she received a favorable ruling from the pope in just six weeks' time. In gratitude, she commissioned a statue of the Virgin Mary holding the baby Jesus. As promised, she called the statue Our Lady of Prompt Succor and in 1810 brought it with her to New Orleans, where it was placed in the convent's chapel.

Our Lady of Prompt Succor is the patroness of Louisiana and New Orleans.

Her feast day is January 8 and is always celebrated with the thanksgiving mass the mother superior had promised for winning the Battle of New Orleans.

During the Battle of New Orleans, the citizens of the city became truly aware of the intercessionary powers of this aspect of Mary. Louisiana had been purchased from France by the United States in 1803, but during the War of 1812 the young nation and Britain fought a second war that lasted about two years. During the last weeks of 1814, the British threatened to attack and loot New Orleans. General Andrew Jackson led a smaller force of several thousand troops, mostly militiamen and volunteers, against a much larger army of experienced regular British soldiers; the people feared total defeat and destruction. By January 1815 the British army was sailing into the port and the citizens on land mobilized as best they could to defend their city. The bishop of Louisiana directed the clergy to hold public services in all Catholic churches to pray for God's protection. The Chapel of Our Lady of Consolation at the Ursuline Convent on Chartres Street was filled with praying women and children. On January 7 they prayed before the statue of Our Lady of Prompt Succor for the entire night. The mother superior of the Ursulines made a vow to have a Mass of thanksgiving sung every year if the Americans were victorious. As Mass was being said on January 8 for General Jackson and his troops, it was interrupted by a courier who shouted, "Victory is ours!" The battle had lasted only twenty-five minutes and there was very little loss of life for the Americans.

The mostly Roman Catholic population of New Orleans were not the only ones who credited Our Lady of Prompt Succor for help with the victory. Andrew Jackson himself insisted that the victory was a "signal interposition of heaven." In gratitude he went out of his way to visit the Ursuline nuns at their convent and thank them for their prayer, "Our Lady of Prompt Succor, Hasten to help us!"

Today, this original statue has been placed above the high altar in the shrine on State Street in New Orleans. Devotees from all over the United States visit it and it is a familiar stopping point for most citizens of New Orleans.

Main altar of the Church of Our Lady of Prompt Succor
in New Orleans, Louisiana.

The Sweetheart Statue In the Ursuline Chapel, another statue, much older and smaller can also be found. It also depicts the Virgin Mary holding Jesus as a baby. She is known as "Sweetheart." Found in the ancient monastery of Pont-St.–Esprit in France, the statue is believed to be at least three hundred years old. The statue was brought to the convent in New Orleans in 1785 by the nun who had rescued it from oblivion in the monastery attic. It was installed in the Ursuline Convent's chapel years before the arrival of the Our Lady of Prompt Succor statue.

In 1812, a great fire broke out in the Old French Quarter in New Orleans and threatened the convent. Most of the nuns and their students were safely evacuated. An elderly nun could not move fast enough, and Mother Saint Michel ran to help her. As the flames neared, she saw that the old nun was clutching the Sweetheart statue. Together the nuns prayed, "Our Lady of Prompt Succor, we are lost if you do not come to our aid." A change in the wind immediately diverted the fire, saving the convent from total destruction.

The Sweetheart is like a family member for Ursuline alumnae. Whenever this country is at war, it is customary for the academy's former students who have families in the armed forces to pray to the Sweetheart for their safe return. She is considered an early image of Our Lady of Prompt Succor. Like the larger statue, the Sweetheart depicts Mary and Jesus with crowns on their heads. As Mary supports Jesus and holds him up as if she is offering him to us, Jesus supports a globe of the entire world in his hand. This is a common image in ecclesiastical art in both painting and statuary. It reminds the world of how dependent the Christ Child was on His mother and how His love for humankind and the world is as open, innocent, and all-accepting as a child's.

The "Sweetheart Statue" was brought to the Ursaline Convent in New Orleans in 1785.

Hail Mary Full of Grace! the Lord is with you; Blessed are you among women, and blessed is the fruit of your womb Jesus. Holy Mary, Mother of God, pray for us sinners, now and at the hour of our death. Amen.

Catherine heard the rustle of a silk dress and a beautiful woman sat down in the Father Director's chair next to her. The woman was dressed in an ivory-colored dress with a blue mantle and a white veil covering her head and draping over her shoulders.

Our Lady of Grace

Alhough the Miraculous Medal is worn almost as often as a crucifix by Roman Catholics, few realize that the designs on the front and back owe their inspiration to a series of apparitions of the Virgin Mary.

It is said that the year 1830 announced the dawning of the Marian era. Until then, the last Church-sanctioned apparition of Mary was of Our Lady of Guadalupe in Mexico almost three hundred years before. Within that time frame, the entire religious world of western Europe was shaken to its core by the upheaval of the Reformation, Counter-Reformation, and the French Revolution. In France, religious worship was demonized, and the clergy was ostracized as ancient monasteries and artworks were destroyed.

On the night of July 18, 1830, in the Motherhouse of the Sisters of Charity in Paris, a barely literate twenty-four-year-old novice named Catherine Laboure was shaken from her sleep by a beautiful five-year-old boy. Catherine was in her curtained bed in a dormitory with other novices. Shocked at the dazzling garments the child wore, she was certain the other nuns would wake up.

IMMACOLATA CONCEZIONE

"Catherine," said the boy. "Come to the chapel; the Blessed Virgin is waiting for you."

Catherine was too shocked to speak but thought the words, "But I shall be heard."

The child calmly spoke, "Be calm, it is half past eleven, everyone is asleep; come, I am waiting for you."

Catherine dressed quickly and followed the child. As they reached the chapel, the door opened at the light touch of his finger. The room was glowing in light as all of the candles were lit as if for Midnight Mass. Catherine knelt to pray.

As it neared midnight, the child said, "Here is the Blessed Virgin!"

Catherine heard the rustle of a silk dress and a beautiful woman sat down in the Father Director's chair next to her. The woman was dressed in an ivory-colored dress with a blue mantle and a white veil covering her head and draping over her shoulders. Her hands radiated beams of light, the color of jewels.

In a much stronger voice, the child said, "Here is the Blessed Virgin."

Catherine knelt in front of the woman, putting her hands in her lap as she looked into the woman's eyes. In her own words, Catherine later recounted, "I do not know how long I remained there; it seemed but a moment, but the sweetest of my life."

When the Virgin Mary spoke, she said, "The good God, my child, wishes to entrust you with a mission. It will be the cause of much suffering to you, but you will overcome this, knowing that what you do is for the glory of God. You will be contradicted, but you will have the grace to bear it; do not fear! You will see certain things; give an account of them. You will be inspired in your prayers. Tell with confidence all that passes within you. Tell it with simplicity. Have confidence. Do not be afraid."

Mary then went on to relate the misfortunes that were about to befall France and the rest of the world. When Catherine wondered to herself when these things were to happen, "I understood clearly, *forty years*."

The Virgin ended the conversation by saying, "Come to the foot of this altar; there, graces will be poured on all those who ask for them with confidence and fervor. They will be poured out on the great and the humble." And in Catherine's words, "the Virgin disappeared like a light is extinguished."

The child then led Catherine back to bed, where she remained awake for the entire night, wondering exactly what her mission would be.

Catherine did not see Mary again until November 27, 1830, which was the Saturday before the first Sunday of Advent. Though she was with other nuns in the chapel at the 5:30 p.m. prayers, Catherine was the only one who saw the apparition. At the point reserved for interior meditation, when the chapel was at its quietest, Catherine heard the sound of the rustling silk.

In her words, "When I looked in that direction, I saw the Blessed Virgin. She was standing, dressed in a white robe of silk, like the dawn, her feet resting on a globe, only half of which I could see. In her hands, held at the level of her breast, she held a smaller globe, her eyes raised towards heaven . . . her face was beautiful, I could not describe it . . . Then suddenly, I saw rings on her fingers, covered with jewels, some large and some small, from which came beautiful rays

Detail of altar in a private chapel used by the town residents in Tepotzotlan, Yucatan, Mexico.

...At this moment, when I was contemplating the Virgin, she lowered her eyes and looked at me and an interior voice spoke to me: 'This globe you see represents the entire world, particularly France ... and each person in particular.'"

As Catherine marveled at the beauty of the rays of light exuding from Mary, the voice said, "This is a symbol of the graces which I shed on those who ask me." When Catherine wondered why some of the jewels on Mary were not radiating light like the others, the voice said, "Those jewels which are in shadow represent the graces which people forget to ask me for." Then the apparition changed, and Mary appeared with a white dress, a blue mantle, and a white veil. She was standing on the globe and had one foot on the head of a serpent that lay at her feet. The year 1830 was marked at the globe's base. The Virgin's hands were pointing downward, and a cascade of light rays were falling from her hands onto the globe.

An oval then formed around Mary, and on it were written these words in gold, "O MARY CONCEIVED WITHOUT SIN, PRAY FOR US WHO HAVE RECOURSE TO THEE."

The same interior voice said, "Have a medal struck after this model. Those who

The Virgin Mary
in Brooklyn, New York.

wear it will receive great graces; abundant graces will be given to those who have confidence." As the voice faded out, the oval turned and Catherine saw what was on the reverse of the medal: The letter *M* surmounted by a bar and a cross; beneath the *M* were the hearts of Jesus and Mary, the one crowned with thorns, the other pierced with a sword. Encircling these symbols were twelve stars.

For the next year, Catherine saw this vision six times. Having little contact with the outside world and feeling pressured to complete her mission, she told her spiritual director, Father John Marie Aladel, about the Virgin's mandate. Just as Mary predicted in the first vision, he did not believe her. As she persisted to repeat her story to him throughout the year, he and Catherine had many stormy disagreements. At his request, she wrote out a detailed report of what happened. At a loss about what to do with this young girl who not only had these visions, but was so insistent upon having this medal struck, Father Aladel visited the archbishop of Paris in 1832. Having a special devotion to the Virgin Mary, the archbishop did not share Father Aladel's

skepticism and he immediately gave permission to create the medal.

In June 1832, fifteen hundred copies of the medal then known as the Medal of the Immaculate Conception were created. By 1836 more than two million medals had been produced. Because of the many stories of cures, wonders, and death-bed conversions attributed to the medal, it gradually became known as the Miraculous Medal.

Catherine Laboure never revealed to anyone but her spiritual director that it was she who received the visions that caused the medal's creation, and she could never be induced to attend any of the canonical hearings investigating the apparitions. Eventually, this visit of the Virgin Mary was sanctified and officially recognized by the Church based on the miraculous effects of the medals. For the next forty-six years of her life, Catherine nursed the sick and tended the chickens at the Sisters of Charity residence outside of Paris. Her fellow sisters found her "cold and apathetic" and were quite shocked upon learning that it was this obscure, forgettable person whom the Virgin Mary entrusted with her mission. She died on December 31, 1876, and is buried in the convent chapel in Paris, where the Blessed Virgin Mary first appeared to her.

The Symbols on the Medal On the front of the medal, Mary stands alone with her foot crushing the head of a serpent. She is the Victorious Woman of Genesis (Genesis 3:15), where God says to the serpent, "I will put enmities between you and the woman." In Catholic art, Mary is frequently depicted crushing the head of a serpent that represents Satan. In this way, Mary as the highest developed form of human life is shown triumphing over evil. It is believed that the date 1830 at the base of the medal signifies the advent of the Marian age, when apparitions of Mary were to intensify and become more

Hail Mary Full of Grace! the Lord is with you; Blessed are you among women, and blessed is the fruit of your womb Jesus. Holy Mary, Mother of God, pray for us sinners, now and at the hour of our death. Amen.

frequent. Mary is standing on the globe of the world, which gives her spiritual dominion with the title Queen of Heaven and Earth. Brilliant rays of light cascade to earth from Mary's hand. She is showering the world with grace from God. This is where her titles Mediatrix and Advocate for Humanity come from. She is so filled with God's grace and love she needs to share it with others. She looks upon all humankind as her children and tries to show them the path to light and God as any mother would. The words around the frame of the medal, "O Mary conceived without sin, pray for us who have recourse to thee," is a brief prayer in itself. In it we are recognizing Mary's help in interceding for us with God and the belief that she was the only human creature to ever be conceived without original sin.

The imagery on the back of the medal is equally symbolic. There is a cross on the back with a bar through its base. This symbolizes the foot of the Cross. This bar runs through the letter *M*, which stands for both Mary and Mother. This signifies that Mary as Christ's mother stood at the foot of his Cross while he endured his Crucifixion. Beneath the *M* are two hearts, one with thorns running through it (this is the Sacred Heart of Jesus); and the other with a sword in it (the Immaculate Heart of Mary). One of the Seven Sorrows of Mary predicted by the prophesy of Holy Simeon is "the Mother pierced with a sword of sorrow beneath the cross so that the thoughts of many hearts may be revealed" (according to Luke 2:34–35: "you yourself a sword may pierce"). Because Mary had to endure the great sorrow of watching her only son die a humiliating and tortuous death, many on Earth look to her for comfort in their own troubles. They know that she went through the worst agonies a mother could withstand and triumphed over them. Both hearts are equal in size, and both hearts are inflamed by ardent love. Encircling the cross, the *M,* and the two hearts are twelve stars. In art, Mary is frequently depicted crowned by twelve stars. It is believed that the Twelve Apostles looked to her quiet devotion and acceptance of her son's fate for spiritual inspiration. Stars also pertain to the book of Revelation (Apocalypse) as a reference to the "great sign" described as "a woman clothed with the sun, with the moon under her feet, and on her head a crown of twelve stars" (Revelation 12:1). In the Miraculous Medal lie the symbols of Mary's role in salvation from Genesis to Apocalypse. As the Victorious Woman she is destined to take part in the final defeat of the devil.

The Miraculous Medal is considered a physical manifestation of the gift of grace, which exudes from the Virgin Mary. It is considered Mary's token reminder that she is always ready to offer assistance.

Our Lady of the Miraculous Medal is the patroness of France.

The feast day of Our Lady of the Miraculous Medal is the same day as the Feast of the Immaculate Conception, December 8.

Upon closer inspection, the light took on a form and the figure of a beautiful woman weeping could be made out. The woman was sitting on a rock with her face buried in her hands.

Our Lady of La Salette

One of the most controversial of the Church-approved apparitions of Mary is her visit to La Salette in the French Alps. The seers who saw her were two poor shepherd children, half wild, unwanted by their parents and unschooled. They had little credibility with the people in their region and even less with the local clergy. Yet because of the complete conversion or change of heart of the little town, this apparition was approved within four years.

On September 19, 1846, two shepherds, fourteen-year-old Melanie Calvat and eleven-year-old Maximin Giraud were tending their cows in the Alpine hamlet of La Salette, France, approximately six thousand feet above sea level. Both children had only recently met; the younger of the two, Maximin, was outgoing and friendly. He had insisted on their working together in order to stave off the boredom and loneliness of their tedious job. Melanie Calvat begrudgingly accepted his company. She was known to have a difficult and taciturn nature. She had worked as a shepherd from the time of her tenth birthday, and her master considered her disobedient and lazy. She was the fourth of ten children, and many people in the village remembered her mother as abusive and violent.

NOSTRA Sᴬ DELLA SALETTE.

Verlag von Serz & Cᵒ in Nürnberg.

On this Saturday afternoon in September the children had only been working together for a few days. They had taken a nap after lunch and upon awakening realized that their cows had wandered off. As they scrambled up into the pasture to retrieve them, they saw what seemed to them to be a globe of fire near a little hollow, which looked "as though the sun had fallen on that spot." Upon closer inspection, the light took on a form and the figure of a beautiful woman weeping could be made out. The woman was sitting on a rock with her face buried in her hands. She saw the children and got up, saying, "Come near, my children, do not be afraid. I am here to tell you great news."

Reassured and extremely curious, Maximin and Melanie ran over to the woman. They later reported that she was tall and everything about her radiated light. She wore clothing typical of the women of that area; a long dress with an apron, and a shawl crossed over her breast and tied around her back. Her dress, however, was studded in pearls, and her bonnet was a strange crown-shaped hat that exuded bright rays. Hanging from her neck she wore a large crucifix with a figure of Christ on it. Beneath the arms of the cross there were, to the left, a hammer, and to the right, pincers. An even brighter radiance emanated from this crucifix. There were garlands of roses around her head, the edge of her shawl, and around her feet. Throughout her conversation with the children the woman continually wept.

She said: "If my people will not obey, I shall be compelled to loose my Son's arm. It is so heavy, so pressing that I can no longer restrain it. How long I have suffered for you! If my Son is not to cast you off, I am obliged to entreat Him without ceasing. But you take no least notice of that. No matter how well you pray in the future, no matter how well you act, you will never be able to make up to me what I have endured for your sake."

Then the woman pointed out that no one in the village took Sunday off from work. She added, "The cart drivers cannot swear without bringing in my Son's name. These are the two things which make my Son's arms so burdensome."

She went on to say that if the village continued to act impiously there would be a great famine coming and it would be the people's own fault. She added that if the people would change their ways, the rocks would become piles of wheat and the potatoes would sow themselves. Melanie later reported that since the lady was speaking French and she was not familiar with the French word for "potato," the lady stopped what she was saying and added, "Ah, but you do not speak French!" and she continued her dialogue with them in the local patois. She then gave each child a secret that the other could not hear. She questioned them on whether they said their prayers. When they answered "no," she said, "Ah, my children, it is very important to say them, at night and in the morning. When you don't have time at least say an 'Our Father' and a 'Hail Mary.' When you can, say more." She continued in a tearful voice: "Only a few old women go to Mass in the summer. All the rest work every Sunday throughout the summer. And in winter, when they don't know what to do with themselves, they go to mass only to poke fun at religion. During Lent they flock to the butcher shop like dogs."

The lady went on to ask if either of them had ever seen spoiled grain before. Maximin quickly answered, "No."

The lady reminded him that this was not so, "But my child, you must have seen it once near Coin, with your papa. The owner of a field said to your papa, 'Come and see my spoiled grain.' The two of you went. You took two or three ears of grain in your fingers. You rubbed them, and they crumbled to dust. Then you came back from Coin. When you were but a half hour away from Corps, your papa gave you a piece of bread and said, 'Well, my son, eat some bread this year, anyhow. I don't know who will be eating any next year, if the grain goes on spoiling like that.'"

Maximin immediately recalled this experience but was astounded as to how this lady could know it.

In French the lady said, "My children, you will make this known to all my people." She turned from them and started to glide away. She stopped and paused, repeating one more time, "My children, you will make this known to all my people."

The children returned with their cows at the end of the day. Melanie was not inclined to tell anyone of their adventure with the lady. Maximin, however, told his employer all about it. When both children were questioned independently, they told the same story. The priest and the town officials were doubtful. To them, these were just two ignorant children making up a fantasy. But there was

Hail Mary Full of Grace! the Lord is with you; Blessed are you among women, and blessed is the fruit of your womb Jesus. Holy Mary, Mother of God, pray for us sinners, now and at the hour of our death. Amen.

something in the tone of the story that affected the people of the town. This lady was not using religious metaphors, she was speaking in an accessible, straightforward manner. When the villagers went to visit the spot where the lady appeared, a spring had started flowing. It was thought at first that this was a coincidence, since it had rained the day before and it was common for small springs to appear for a day or so then dry up. But this spring behaved differently, freely flowing no matter what the weather. People who drank from the spring reported dramatic healing activity. The demeanor of the village totally changed. By 1846, France, once a nation dedicated to the Virgin Mary, was now actively a nation trying to live without religious conviction. In the search for material wealth, spiritual values had fallen by the wayside. Though La Salette had only five hundred inhabitants, they, too, had adopted the slack lifestyle of the bigger cities. The lady was right; religious devotion had become a joke. Recognizing the truth in the lady's examples of their behavior, the village church started to fill up with earnest worshipers, and most of the village began honoring Sunday as the Sabbath. The spring itself became a pilgrimage site with devotees of Mary coming from far distances. It is thought that Mary speaking her final words in French was a message to the French nation to reform themselves and their values. La Salette became an approved apparition in 1851.

The seers of La Salette went on to lead troubled lives. Maximin drifted in and out of employment and died by his fortieth birthday. Melanie became a nun. She reveled in the attention she received for being a visionary and felt neglected by the local clergy. In 1879 she published a book alleging what her secret had been. It was a gruesome description of Satan let loose upon the world in 1864 and predictions of mass destruction and the anti-Christ. Because she had fallen under the influence of apocalyptic books and various conspiracy theorists, her book was thought to be purely imaginative and was not sanctioned by the Church. She continually had a small band of followers who believed in these later visions. She died in 1904.

In 1879 a magnificent basilica, Our Lady of La Salette was consecrated on the site of the apparition.

OUR LADY OF LA SALETTE IS THE PATRONESS OF FRANCE.

The Feast of Our Lady of La Salette is September 19.

A golden cloud came out of the cave and flooded the niche with radiance. Then a lady, young and beautiful, exceedingly beautiful, the like of whom I had never seen, stood on the edge of the niche.

Our Lady of Lourdes

Bernadette Soubirous was an unlikely visionary. Her family had lost their business and were all but homeless. They were reduced to living in a dank former dungeon that had been evacuated by the authorities because it was considered too inhumane to house prisoners. At the age of fourteen Bernadette had not yet received her First Communion because she was considered slow-witted and behind in her catechism studies. On February 11, 1858, the impoverished girl's mother sent her, a sister, and a friend out to look for firewood. So that they would not be accused of stealing, the girls went to the outskirts of town, to an area near the Gave River known as Massabielle. Respectable citizens of the town of Lourdes avoided this place, considering it disgusting because pigs grazed there. According to local legend, it had been a place of pagan worship where ancient evils still lurked; many crossed themselves if they had to pass by it. Bernadette was congenitally ill with asthma, so the two younger girls waded across a mill stream to collect wood on the other side while she stayed behind. Not finding any wood on her side, she began to take off her stockings to join the others. She heard the sound of a storm starting to blow up; as she stood up straight she was puzzled as to why the trees remained totally still.

Domina nostra de Lourdes

Bewildered, Bernadette looked around, and in her own words, "I looked across the millstream to a niche above a cave in the rock of Massabielle. A rosebush on the edge of the niche was swaying in the wind. It was all that moved. All else was still. A golden cloud came out of the cave and flooded the niche with radiance. Then a lady, young and beautiful, exceedingly beautiful, the like of whom I had never seen, stood on the edge of the niche. She smiled and smiled at me, beckoning me to come closer as though she were my mother, and she gave me to understand in my soul that I was not mistaken. The lady was dressed in white, with a white veil on her head, and a blue sash at her waist. A rosary of white beads on a gold chain was on her right arm. On that cold winter's day, her feet were bare, but on each foot was a golden rose radiant with the warmth of summer."

Instinctively, Bernadette reached for her rosary for spiritual protection. But she found she could not lift her arm for the sign of the cross until the lady herself started to cross herself. After they made the sign of the cross together, Bernadette began to pray the rosary. The lady passed the beads through her fingers and silently followed her. When Bernadette had finished, the smiling lady bowed to her and disappeared.

That Sunday, Bernadette returned to the site with a group of friends after Mass. The lady appeared, and Bernadette was the only one who could see or communicate with her. She sprinkled the lady with holy water, saying, "If you come from God, stay. If you don't, go away." The lady laughed and inclined her head to receive more water. Her friends were shocked at the physical transformation of Bernadette. She had fallen into a beautiful rapture without a trace of her asthma. When they threw a stone at her, she did not flinch. Frightened that she might be in danger of losing her mind, they ran to get help. Those who came to their aid were amazed at the incredible change in Bernadette's demeanor. They hardly recognized the rapturously happy, graceful young girl in front of them. A neighbor carried her to her mother's house. Bernadette later said that the lady kept in front of her, slightly above her, only disappearing when Bernadette went inside the house. Her parents were angry with Bernadette for causing such a commotion, but those in the crowd who had witnessed her at the grotto advised them to believe her.

She made her third visit to the grotto on February 18, accompanied by two important women from town who insisted she try and write down everything the lady said. Bernadette began the rosary and the lady appeared, surrounded by light. Bernadette entered the grotto and the lady came down from the niche and stood beside her. When Bernadette asked her to please write down her name and what she wanted, the lady laughed.

For the first time she spoke to Bernadette, "Boulet aoue ra gracia de bie aci penden quinze dias?" she asked in the patois dialect of that region. ("Would you have the grace to come here for fifteen days?") When Bernadette replied that she would have to ask her parents' permission, the lady said, "I do not promise you happiness in this life, but in the next." Then she added, "Go and tell the priests that a chapel must be built here." Smiling, she disappeared.

As news spread through Lourdes about the apparitions, Bernadette's visits to the grotto were accompanied by larger and larger crowds. The civil authorities felt compelled to take action, and Bernadette was detained at the local police station for questioning. When she refused to admit that it was all a hoax or a ploy for attention, they began to threaten her family. The Church was also embarrassed and skeptical of the claims of what they considered to be a

OUR LADY OF LOURDES IS THE PATRONESS OF FRANCE. **The feast day of Our Lady of Lourdes is February 11.**

superstitious girl. They had no intention of giving these apparitions any credence. Bernadette never speculated on the lady's identity, she always referred to her as Aquero, the patois word for indescribable being.

It was on February 25, during the ninth apparition, that Bernadette was told to go drink at the spring and wash in it. Thinking that the lady meant the river, Bernadette went toward the Gave but the lady called her back. She pointed at a spot beneath the rock. Bernadette later wrote, "I found some moisture there but it was mud. Three times I threw it away even though the lady said to drink it. Then I washed in it only to have my face besmeared with mud." The large crowd that had gathered started jeering at the girl. Bernadette's aunt, who was among them, was utterly humiliated. She smacked Bernadette in the face saying, "Stop your nonsense!" and sent her home. By the afternoon the muddy area was flowing with pure water. No one in Lourdes had ever seen a spring there before. Many who had been scoffing at Bernadette in the morning were drinking at the spring in the afternoon.

In subsequent apparitions, the lady gave Bernadette a secret prayer to say, which she never revealed to anyone. She asked for penitence and the conversion of sinners. As the crowds grew, the authorities again took Bernadette in for questioning, but she never wavered from her story, always referring to the lady as *Aquero*. In one apparition the lady alighted on a rosebush, and Bernadette feared that the sheer crush of the ever-growing crowd would harm *Aquero*. "I was afraid she might fall, but she kept on smiling at the people. She loved them, and she always seemed sorry to leave them." At the thirteenth visit she repeated her request that Bernadette ask the priest for a procession to the grotto and for a chapel to be built.

Reluctantly, Bernadette returned to Father Peyramale, the village priest. Frustrated and skeptical, he told her that if the lady in white wanted a chapel she should say who she was and she should make the wild rosebush in the niche blossom. It was after this visit that claims of miraculous healing were made by those who drank or washed in the spring. One was a dying two-year-old child who was immersed for fifteen minutes in the water. His family had his coffin prepared on one day and the next he was running around as if he had never been sick. On market day the crowd reached to more than eight thousand people. It was Thursday, March 4, the date of the last of the promised fifteen day visits. All expected something extraordinary to happen. Bernadette's visit with the lady lasted forty-five minutes. When it was over, Bernadette merely extinguished her candle and went home. Nothing dramatic occurred: the rosebush did not bloom, the lady did not announce any message. Bernadette was content, unconcerned about the anticipation and unfulfilled emotions she had aroused in the crowd. For the next three weeks, she later wrote, "The people pestered me, the police watched me, and the public prosecutor almost crushed me." Her family was continually harassed by the town authorities, and Bernadette was threatened with jail if she ever returned to the grotto. ("They forgot I was living in an unused police lockup with the entire family in one room.")

On the night of March 24, she awoke with the familiar urge to return. At five in the morning of March 25, the Feast of the Annunciation, Bernadette returned to the grotto where the lady in white was waiting for her. Bernadette asked her identity several times. The lady only smiled. Finally, the fourth time she asked, "*Aquero* extended her hands toward the ground, swept them upwards to join them on her heart, raised her eyes, but not her head to heaven, leaned tenderly towards me and said, *'Que soy era Immaculada Conceptiou.'* (I am the Immaculate Conception.) She smiled at me. She disappeared. I was alone."

According to Bernadette, she had no idea what the lady meant when she said those words. She had to repeat them to herself over and over in order to remember them for the priest. Father Peyramale was astounded at this announcement. The Catholic tradition that Mary had been conceived without original sin so that she might be worthy to be the Mother of God had only been defined as church doctrine in 1854. It was scarcely an expression common to the average person of Lourdes, much less a girl of Bernadette's social stature. Father Peyramale became Bernadette's greatest defender as she had to face the onslaught of examinations by government officials, medical personnel, and church hierarchy. Regardless of threats, ridicule, and coercion, she never once altered her account of her story to any of them: "I do not ask you to believe, I only told you what I had seen." Three eminent Parisian doctors declared that she was mentally and emotionally sound but that she suffered from asthma. ("My mother could have told them that and saved them the trouble.")

The authorities closed down the grotto and threatened anyone visiting it with arrest. Attempts were made to have Bernadette committed to an insane asylum. Father Peyramale put an end to them by saying, "I know my duty as pastor of my parish and protector of my flock. Your own doctors find no abnormality in Bernadette. You will have to fell me to the ground, pass over my dead body and trample it underfoot, before you touch a hair of the child's head."

"Les Piscines et Le Gave," Lourdes, France.

On July 16, Bernadette saw the lady in white for the last time. Since the grotto was off-limits, she knelt in the meadow on the far side of the river. "I began my rosary and my lady stood in the grotto smiling at me. It was the Feast of Our Lady of Mount Carmel. She looked more beautiful than I had ever seen her. This would be the last time I would see her on this earth. . . . She left heaven in my heart and it has been there ever since."

A church commission was set up to investigate the claims of miraculous healing by the spring water. Public opinion forced the reopening of the grotto, and it was approved as a shrine in 1862. Instead of a little chapel, a major basilica, Our Lady of Lourdes, was built on the site. Millions of pilgrims come every year, and it is the world's most visited site dedicated to the Virgin Mary.

Bernadette eventually joined the Sisters of Nevers to avoid the attention her presence created. Her Mother Superior disliked her and forbade her from ever mentioning the apparitions. Although her health steadily declined, she never took any interest in the healing powers of the water at the grotto. Bernadette's written account of the apparitions shows Mary in a very light and loving manner. Like many visionaries, Bernadette enjoyed no special favors in this world. She remained sick all her life and died in 1879 at the age of thirty-five. When her body was exhumed in 1908, it was found to be uncorrupted. She was recognized as a saint by the Catholic Church in 1933.

Our Lady of Lourdes is depicted in white with a blue sash, holding a rosary. Bernadette always felt that Church-sanctioned artistic images of Mary in this apparition were totally wrong, insisting that the lady she saw was a young one, between the ages of twelve and fourteen.

There are four traditional gifts imparted by a pilgrimage to Lourdes: **(1) The gift of the miraculous water, (2) the gift of healing, (3) the gift of reconciliation, and (4) the gift of friendship.**

FOLLOWING PAGES: Outdoor shrine for Our Lady of Lourdes in Brooklyn, New York.

It is said that Our Lady of Perpetual Help never refuses a request, no matter how small or frivolous it may seem. Many who have felt unworthy to call on her in their direst need report hearing a calm voice saying, "Why don't you just ask?"

Our Lady of Perpetual Help

Icons are visual prayers. Artists who painted them were usually monks who spent whole days in contemplation, meditating on the mysteries of God. In the East, icons not only serve as instructive visual stories but because of the spiritual atmosphere in which they are channeled, they are also venerated along with the word of God. *Our Lady of Perpetual Help* is an icon whose style bridges both Eastern and Western Churches. Its subject is called the Virgin of the Passion, because it deals with Mary's role in the Crucifixion of Christ. Like most of these works, the artist is anonymous but most likely came out of the Andrea Rizo de Candia (1422–1499) school of Crete. This mesmerizing picture, which spent years in anonymity, is now venerated and honored in all corners of the world and enjoys universal devotion.

Written remembrances of the image date back to the 1400s, when it was venerated in a church on the island of Crete as *The Miraculous Picture of the Mother of God*. In the late 1490s, a local merchant aware of all the wondrous stories surrounding the icon, stole it and took it with him to Rome. During the voyage over, a violent storm terrified the crew. Aware that the merchant was traveling with the painting, they had him take it out for them to pray in front of. They attributed their safe crossing to the intercession of the Virgin in the picture. While in Rome, the merchant became mortally ill. Repenting of his theft, he asked the friend he was staying with to promise to see that the painting was given to a church. The friend agreed and took the painting upon the merchant's death. However, the man's wife was so charmed by the image, she hung it in her bedroom and the merchant's request was never honored. Mary appeared twice to the family's six-year-old daughter, and it was in these visions that she first announced herself as Our Lady of

Our Lady of Perpetual Help.

Perpetual Help. She asked that the family stop hoarding the picture and give it to a church that was located between Santa Maria Maggiore and San Giovanni in Laterano. After consulting with a priest, the family gave the painting to the Church of San Matteo, an obscure, out-of-the-way parish. It was installed on March 27, 1499. Almost immediately, pilgrims from all walks of life came to seek comfort in contemplation in front of the icon. For the next three hundred years, the painting known as *The Madonna di San Matteo*, remained undisturbed as it acquired a loyal group of devotees. In 1798, Napoléon's troops conquered Rome, and San Matteo was one of the thirty churches destroyed by the French army. The Irish Augustinian monks who were in charge of the church brought the icon to the Monastery of Saint Mary in Posterula in the Trastevere section of Rome and placed it in a private chapel. Its existence was all but forgotten as the original band of monks from San Matteo were dispersed to Ireland and America.

Michael Marchi, an altar boy who served Mass at Saint Mary in Posterula remembered one of the last of the old monks: "This good brother used to tell me with a certain air of mystery and anxiety, especially during the years 1850 and 1851, these precise words, 'Make sure you know, my son, that the image of the Virgin of Saint Matthew is upstairs in the chapel; don't ever forget it . . . do you understand? It is a miraculous picture.' At that time the brother was almost totally blind."

Michael Marchi entered into religious life, taking orders in the Redemptorist Missionaries. In 1855 they purchased Villa Caserta in Rome to house their order. What they did not realize was, that this estate had been built over the ruins of the Monastery and Church of San Matteo. An investigation into the history of the property turned up writings about an ancient icon of the Mother of God that had enjoyed "great veneration and fame for its miracles," which was once housed in San Matteo. In 1863 a famous Jesuit preacher came and gave a sermon about the now lost icon of *The Virgin of Perpetual Help*. Father Marchi realized this was the same dust-laden picture he had always seen above the altar of the house chapel of the Augustinian Fathers at Saint Mary in Posterula.

"There was no devotion to it, no decorations, not even a lamp to acknowledge its presence . . . it remained covered with dust and practically abandoned, many were the times when I served Mass there, that I would stare at it with great attention."

This providential discovery came to the attention of Pope Pius IX, who

OUR LADY OF PERPETUAL HELP IS THE PATRONESS OF HAITI AND ITALY. **The feast day of Our Lady of Perpetual Help is June 27.**

remembered praying before the image in San Matteo as a boy. He ordered that the icon of *Our Lady of Perpetual Help* be brought to the new church of Saint Alfonso for public veneration. Situated on the Esquiline Hill, this is the exact location, between the two basilicas of Santa Maria Maggiore and San Giovanni in Laterano, that the Virgin Mary had originally requested for it to be placed. Pilgrims come from all over the world to be in the presence of the icon.

The pope did not give the Redemptorists the icon just to keep in their church for visiting pilgrims, but rather to make it their mission to disseminate this image of Mary throughout the world. Copies of this icon are considered just as capable of working miracles as the original. Shrines and legions of devotees to Our Lady of Perpetual Help can be found in the United States, Haiti, Ecuador, Peru, Suriname, Chile, Brazil, Mexico, Ireland, Italy, Poland, France, Spain, Singapore, and the Philippines.

Mary is the largest figure in this icon, but the focal point or center of the picture is her hand being clutched by her Son's. Jesus is a young boy who has just run to his mother in such a fright that one of His sandals is dangling off his feet. Mary calmly shields Him, confident of her power to protect and comfort Him. On either side of them are the objects of the Child's fear. The archangels Gabriel and Michael have revealed to Him the Cross, the spear, and the sponge, foreshadowing his future torment and execution. Since the birth of her Son, Mary knew He was destined to suffer and die for humankind, yet she firmly believed in His redemption. Therefore, she was able to calm the Child Jesus in this moment of anxiety. If God Himself can reach out to Mary for refuge, then anyone is able to approach her, no matter what we fear, our future or our past actions. Regardless how we judge ourselves, she has total belief and faith in us. Greek letters on either side of Mary's head are abbreviations for the title, "Mother of God." Beside the head of Jesus are the Greek letters for "Jesus Christ." It is important to note that Mary is not holding Jesus's hand in a tight grip but she leaves it open in invitation to the viewer to join them. Jesus has his hand palm turned down into His mother's. This symbolizes the grace and favors that He distributes through her intercession. Mary looks directly at the viewer, offering love and comfort to all who gaze at the image.

It is said that Our Lady of Perpetual Help never refuses a request, no matter how small or frivolous it may seem. Many who have felt unworthy to call on her in their direst need report hearing a calm voice saying, "Why don't you just ask?"

Not only was it worm-eaten, but the face of the Madonna was that of a course, rough, country-woman …a piece of canvas was missing just above her head … her mantle was cracked.

Our Lady of Pompeii

Bartolo Longo wrote about his great disappointment upon being given the miraculous painting of Our Lady of the Rosary:

Not only was it worm-eaten, but the face of the Madonna was that of a course, rough, country-woman …a piece of canvas was missing just above her head …her mantle was cracked. Nothing need be said of the hideousness of the other figures. St. Dominic looked like a street idiot. To Our Lady's left was a Saint Rose. This I had changed later into a Saint Catherine of Siena. . . . I hesitated whether to refuse the gift or to accept. . . . I took it.

Bought in a junk shop for less than a dollar, the painting was kept in a convent. Its reluctant recipient had promised to bring a painting to a prayer meeting he was sponsoring in the dilapidated town of Valle di Pompei. It was so artistically inferior that he accepted it only so as not to insult the mother superior of the convent. She told him, "Take it with you, you will see that the Blessed Mother will use this painting to work many miracles." Little did he realize the extent of transformation it would bring to the town, its residents, and the world.

Bartolo Longo was born in 1841, the child of a well-to-do family. As a law student at the University of Naples, he was swept up in the wave of anticlericalism then popular among the intelligentsia. He eventually befriended a group of Spiritualists and began attending seances. This led to his being inducted into a satanic cult where he publicly mocked and derided all aspects of the Catholic faith. The frequent fasts and gruesome rituals demanded of him as a priest of Satan weakened his physical and mental health, eventually leading to a nervous breakdown. A law professor noticed Longo's frail physical and emotional state and aided him in his release from the grip of the occult. As his health returned, Longo was introduced to a Dominican priest trained in philosophy and theology. Eventually he was rebaptized as a Catholic, taking the middle name Maria after the Virgin Mary. The history of the Dominican order is based on Saint Dominic's propagation of the rosary. Longo felt the repetitive rhythm of the Hail Mary in the rosary had a calming effect on his spirit and gave him a sense of well-being. He became a Dominican tertiary devoted to teaching the rosary. As a penance for his former life he chose to work in the poor and destitute town of Valle di Pompei.

Located within minutes of the ruins of the ancient city of Pompeii, the little town was founded by Christians three hundred years after the destruction of the ancient city by the cataclysmic eruption of Mount Vesuvius in A.D. 79. In the eleventh century the Benedictine order was entrusted with caring for the large and thriving church that stood within the town. A malaria epidemic all but wiped out the entire population in 1659. The large church was razed and replaced by a smaller one. The land was ceded to a Neapolitan nobleman and left in neglect. Over the years, the remaining residents were considered "superstitious and criminal, many being thieves." When Bartolo Longo arrived to work among the people there in 1872, there was no school and no government representative, and the little church had deteriorated and was infested with rats and lizards. He went door to door to preach the importance of the rosary to little effect. His discouragement turned to suicidal despair as he thought of his past. He wrote:

The feast day for Our Lady of Pompeii is the day for Our Lady of the Rosary, October 7.

"I thought that perhaps as the priesthood of Christ is for eternity, so also the priesthood of Satan is for eternity. So, despite my repentance, I thought that I was still consecrated to Satan, and that I am still his slave and property as he awaits me in Hell. As I pondered over my condition, I experienced a deep sense of despair and almost committed suicide. Then I heard an echo in my ear of the voice of Friar Alberto repeating the words of the Blessed Virgin Mary: 'One who propagates my Rosary shall be saved.'"

Bartolo Longo

He vowed to continue his mission regardless of its apparent failure. He began prayer meetings in the church, which at first were attended only by a few children. His restoration of the little church brought in more people, and he invited the Redemptorist Fathers to hold a two-week mission. He had promised to display a painting of the Virgin Mary for the last evening. The only artwork available to him was the poorly executed work of art that he received from the nuns. On November 13, 1875, *The Queen of the Rosary* arrived in Pompeii wrapped in a sheet on top of a manure pile that was being delivered to a nearby field. The public display of the painting effected immediate changes in the little town. Three hundred families promised a penny a month in order to build a better church to house it. As soon as the cornerstone was laid for the new basilica in May 1876, miraculous healings began taking place at the shrine. In 1880 the painting was restored by the famous Neapolitan painter Federico Maldarelli (1826–1893). The basilica was completed in 1881. The community working and praying together changed the town from a depressed, dangerous, and dirty place to a thriving city. Bartolo Longo went on to found many hospices, orphanages, and devotional societies centered on the healing powers of the rosary. There are churches named after Our Lady of Pompeii all over the world.

This painting, currently on display at the Basilica of Our Lady of Pompeii attracts thousands of pilgrims a day. The image itself depicts Mary as Queen of Heaven. She sits on a throne inside a church with the Christ Child on her lap. She, in turn, becomes the physical throne for Him. The Infant Jesus is handing the rosary to Saint Dominic, the founder of the Dominican Order. Mary is handing a rosary to Saint Catherine of Siena, a Dominican tertiary who is also the patron saint of Italy. Both Saint Dominic and Saint Catherine were mystics who had visions of Mary. The Dominican Order propagates the rosary in the belief it puts one in a higher state of mind and opens one up to grace.

At Pompeii the Virgin Mary worked through the unlikely instruments of a former satanist and a discarded painting. The transformation of the neglected town of Pompeii and its people have inspired all who visit the basilica or read its story.

FOLLOWING PAGES: Laundromat wall in New York City, New York.
PAGES 86–87: Outdoor neighborhood shrine and home altar in Mexico City, Mexico.

Poster for the Mexican release of
Gone With the Wind includes
Our Lady of Guadalupe.
<small>FOLLOWING PAGES</small>: Bedroom
shrine, and The Mother
of Grace Clubhouse, Gloucester,
Massachusetts.

Procession for the blessing
of the fishing boats,
Gloucester, Massachusetts.
FOLLOWING PAGES: private
altars in Havana, Cuba.

FERNANDITO
DE TUS
PADRES

FERNANDITO
DE TU
HERMANA

2 enero 1928

FERNANDO SAINZ de la MAZA
URIARTE

Mary Beirne, who was one of the first to see the vision and who was one of the remaining original witnesses, declared, "I am quite clear about everything I have said, and I make this statement knowing I am going before my God."

Our Lady of Knock

Ireland has been devoted to the Virgin Mary since Saint Patrick first evangelized it in the early part of the first millennium. The abbey he built in Meath, known as Our Lady of Tryme was one of the more famous pilgrimage points in Europe for those seeking Mary's intercession. By the sixth century, while the rest of Europe was being devastated by barbarian hordes, abbeys and monasteries flourished throughout Ireland. The monastic settlements did much to stabilize European culture and the Irish have been credited with saving Western civilization. Most of these monasteries had strong devotions to Mary, the monks frequently dedicating their work to her. In 1688 when Catholic King James II of England, Scotland, and Ireland was overthrown by Protestant William and Mary, Catholicism was outlawed in Ireland and most of the early shrines to Mary were destroyed. English settlers took over Irish lands, and a strict penal code was established against the mostly Catholic population. They were not free to practice their religion again until 1829. Half the population of Ireland either emigrated or died of starvation in the great famine of the 1840s.

Despite the horrendous suffering inflicted on the Irish throughout their history, their admiration of the Virgin Mary as an example of human endurance has always remained constant. When Mary appeared at Knock in 1879, she remained completely silent. She had no predictions or warnings to make, but the people got her message. Though they were going through terrible times, she was with them.

For the residents of Knock ("Cnoc Mhuire"—Mary's Hill), a village in

County Mayo, 1879 looked to be a bad year. The potato crop was again threatened with blight, rents were driven up, and many families faced evictions. In the face of this desperation, the pastor of Knock began a series of one hundred masses. On August 21, 1879, the last mass was said. That evening during a pouring rain, two women coming from their chores saw a light emanating from the village church, Saint John the Baptist. A farmer noticed that the sky over the church was starry and clear, despite the rain everywhere else. An elderly woman started yelling, "The Blessed Virgin!" Those who ran to the church all agreed upon what they saw. On the wall of the church was an apparition of a living tableau of the Virgin Mary: wearing white garments and a brilliant crown on her head, with a rose under the crown on the forehead, she was prayerfully raising her eyes to heaven. Saint Joseph stood on Mary's right with his head inclined toward her. On the left of Mary was Saint John the Evangelist, vested as a bishop, his left hand holding an open book and his right hand raised in preaching. To the left of Saint John, a cross and a lamb were on top of an altar. Overhead, angels hovered above the lamb. Mary Beirne, a sixteen-year-old girl, cried out, "Oh look at the statues! Why didn't the priest tell us he bought new statues for the church!" When the figures began to move, the witnesses to this vision—men, women, teenagers, and children—began reciting the rosary in the pouring rain. They later testified that the vision lasted two hours. Others in the village who were not at the site reported seeing a strange light coming from the church. When an elderly woman tried to touch Mary, she smiled at her but receded away. Despite the heavy rain, the ground under and around the apparition was completely dry.

A church inquiry was set up by Archbishop Gilmartin of Tuam to investigate the apparition. As word spread of Mary's visit, pilgrims began arriving in Knock. Within the first ten days of the appearance, the first miraculous healing, that of a

OUR LADY OF KNOCK IS THE PATRONESS OF IRELAND. **The feast day of Our Lady of Knock is August 21.**

young girl born deaf, was recorded. Others who claimed a cure left their crutches and canes at the site, many of these were then attached to the wall. It was not uncommon for pilgrims to chip plaster off the wall as a souvenir. On January 6, 1880, while the first inquiry was taking place, the same apparition occurred in front of a larger crowd. This happened again on February 10 and 12 of that year. By the end of 1880, three hundred cures had been recorded by the village priest. One of the pilgrims, who had been cured soon after the apparition, testified many years later that he had seen "as many as half-a-dozen pilgrims simultaneously undergoing their cure or getting relief, and in vision I see the lame walk, my case included, the sightless seeing, the withered skins expanding." Archbishop Lynch of Toronto, Canada, was among those who had been healed at the shrine. He then led pilgrimages from North America to the little village.

Because of the presence of angels in the apparition, Mary is sometimes given her ancient title, Mary, Queen of the Angels, when people refer to this visit. In 1936, a commission investigating the events of 1879 still had access to many of the original seers. Mary Beirne, who was one of the first to see the vision and who was one of the remaining original witnesses, declared, "I am quite clear about everything I have said, and I make this statement knowing I am going before my God." Throughout the years, none of the original witnesses had ever changed or embellished their story. There were no "deathbed confessions" of fraud. Attempts made to re-create the visions by use of magic lanterns and projection devices were all unsuccessful. Like most places where Mary appeared, the local people did not care if the church officials believed them or not. They knew what they saw.

Today, Knock is one of the officially recognized apparitions of Mary. As many as 1.5 million pilgrims visit the little church every year.

I promise salvation to those who embrace devotion to my Immaculate Heart. Their souls will be loved by God as flowers placed by me to adorn His throne. These souls will suffer a great deal but I will never leave them. My Immaculate Heart will be their refuge, the way that will lead them to God.

Our Lady of Fatima

The twentieth century was the first time in history where we had the ability to destroy not only the entire human race but all other forms of life on this planet. During World War I, the violence of which people had never seen before, Mary came to Fatima, Portugal, with a very serious warning. Expressing the belief that humankind had drifted away from God, she wanted the world to offer up reparations for the disastrous state of the earth. Fatima is the most prophetic of Mary's apparitions. She correctly foretold the suffering imposed by the Communist states and the carnage of World War II. The third secret of Fatima was deemed too terrifying to release. It was finally revealed by the Vatican on May 13, 2000, in the hopes that what it had predicted had passed. Others strongly disagree with the Vatican's interpretation and insist it is a portent of the end of the world. Our Lady of Fatima is an angry, pained mother, demanding that her children take action before it is too late.

It is said that Mary usually appears to the simplest and least complicated of people because they do not try to judge or interpret what she says, they merely report it. For this reason, many times her visionaries are children. In 1916, a nine-year-old girl from Fatima named Lucia dos Santos was out tending sheep with her two younger cousins, Francisco and Jacinta. They were happily playing a little game with stones when they saw an immense light come from the sky in their direction. At the center of the light was a translucent angelic form.

"Do not be afraid!" he said. "I am the Angel of Peace. Pray with me." Kneeling, he bowed down until his forehead touched the ground. He taught them a prayer that he made

NOSTRA SIGNORA DI FATIMA

them repeat three times. "My God, I believe, I adore, I trust and I love You! I ask pardon of You for those who do not believe, do not adore, do not trust and do not love You." Rising, he told them, "Pray thus. The hearts of Jesus and Mary are attentive to the words of your prayers."

This was not the first time Lucia had seen this angel. When she had previously tended sheep with other companions, she had witnessed the light of the angel overhead. When her friends had told their parents what they had seen, they were all accused of fabricating a story out of boredom. Because of this, Lucia convinced her younger cousins to keep the angelic visit a secret. All three children began praying in the manner taught to them by the angel. Toward the end of summer they received another visit from the angel, admonishing them for frittering away so much time in play. He told them he was Guardian Angel of Portugal and that God was offended by the sins of others. He advised the children to pray more and "Above all, accept and bear with submission, all the suffering which the Lord allows in your lives. In this way you will draw down peace upon your country." Before winter came they received one more visit from this angel in which he told them that Jesus Christ was outraged by ungrateful and indifferent men. He implored them to keep praying and gave them Communion.

The children continued to work, play, and pray together throughout the winter months. On Sunday, May 13, 1917, they were leading their flocks to a grazing field called the Cova da Iria. They were frightened by flashes of lightning and were shocked to see a beautiful lady who glowed brighter than the sun. When she spoke to them, Lucia was the only one who could hear her, "Fear not, I will not harm you. I am from heaven."

When Lucia asked her what it was she wanted, the lady answered, "I ask you to come here for six consecutive months, on the thirteenth day at this same hour. I will tell you later who I am and why I have come to you. I shall return here again a seventh time."

Lucia asked if they could go to heaven with the lady, and she was told that they would all come to heaven with her but that "Francisco must pray many rosaries." The lady added, "Let him pray the rosary. In that way he too will be able to see me." Francisco had only seen Lucia talking to a bright light. He said one decade of the rosary, and he, too, was able to see the lady. Streams of light radiated onto the children from the lady's hands. As she left them, she told the children, "Say the rosary every day to earn peace for the world and the end of the war."

Lucia's family and friends greeted her story about the lady with scorn and mockery. Her cousins had a different experience. Their father, believing that they truly had some sort of celestial vision, protected and respected them. On June 13 about fifty people accompanied the children to the Cova da Iria. Lucia called Jacinta out of a group of playing children. Lightning had started to flash even though it was a beautiful day. Lucia, Jacinta, and Francisco ran toward the

JACINTA MARTO   FRANCISCO MARTO

oak tree where they had seen the lady a month before. Though others in the crowd could not see her, some reported hearing a "buzzing noise" or a "tiny little voice." The lady, enveloped in a mystical light, taught the children a prayer, and made the following promise to the world, "I promise salvation to those who embrace devotion to my Immaculate Heart. Their souls will be loved by God as flowers placed by me to adorn His throne. These souls will suffer a great deal but I will never leave them. My Immaculate Heart will be their refuge, the way that will lead them to God." She again showered the children with light from her hands. People in the crowd heard a "rushing sound" and the three children shouted, "There she goes, there she goes!" as they pointed to the sky in the east. To everyone's amazement, the branches of the tree, which had been standing straight up a few minutes before, were also pointing to the east.

The third visit, which took place on July 13, was attended by thousands of believers, cynics, and those searching for miracles. Lucia has written that between the past month and this day she was continually tormented by self-doubt. No one in her immediate family seemed to believe her, perhaps this was all a trick of her mind. The large crowd quieted down as they heard a buzzing sound. A cloud moved in over the oak tree. They watched as Lucia, enraptured, appeared to be having a conversation with the cloud. At one point, the girl cried out in horror. After a few minutes, there was the sound of thunder and the cloud lifted. The children waved good-bye to it. When asked what made her cry out, Lucia said, "It was a secret." In her own memoirs, she wrote that as the lady started to appear all her doubts about whether this was really happening or not left her forever. In this visit, the famous Three Secrets of Fatima were imparted to the children.

The local government looked upon the growing interest in the alleged apparitions in Fatima as a dangerous threat to its sovereignty. The royalists had recently been driven out of government and religion was looked upon as equaling royalism. Many monasteries and parochial schools had been closed down. The prime minister had promised that within twenty years all trace of religion would be gone from Portugal. The fourth apparition of the lady took place on August 13. Almost fifteen thousand people were gathered in the Cova da Iria, but Lucia, Jacinta, and Francisco were locked in the town jail. Even without the seers the crowd witnessed the cloud hovering over the oak tree, there were sounds of explosions, and the ground shook. A mystical light showered the crowd, reflecting all the colors of the rainbow. While this was happening, each of the children were separately questioned for hours. They refused to give up the secrets they were told by the lady. Though each was told that the others had completely recanted their story of the lady, not one of them would change their personal account. As a last resort the mayor told them that obviously there were no secrets, and he was going to boil them in oil if they did not admit the apparitions were all a lie. Instead of collapsing in hysteria, the three remained silent, and the children were released on August 15.

The lady came to them in the area near their village and told them she wanted them to continue their pilgrimages to the Cova da Iria on the thirteenth of the month. She also told them to pray the rosary every day. "Pray. Pray very much, and make sacrifices for sinners. So many souls go to hell because there is no one to pray and to make sacrifices for them." The seriousness with which the children took her words greatly altered their personalities. Neighbors who once mocked them became their biggest defenders.

By the September 13 apparition, there were over thirty thousand people in the Cova da Iria. In the middle of a cloudless sky, many witnessed a luminous globe moving from east to west. According to Lucia, the lady asked the people to pray the rosary to obtain the end of the war. She also promised that she would perform a miracle on her next and last visit so that everyone would believe.

The apparition of October 13 is widely documented and was reported by newspapers all over the world. Even the most anticlerical Portuguese news agencies reported "strange natural phenomena" that had occurred in front of a crowd of at least fifty thousand people. Despite heavy rains, pilgrims arrived to the little town, most of them on foot. A few minutes before 1:30 in the afternoon it stopped raining. What happened next has been detailed by news reporters (most of whom were extremely skeptical of the children), eyewitnesses in the crowd, professors from the university, government officials, and even those who lived miles away. The sun appeared through the clouds, shone very brightly, and began to tremble and dance, whirling through the sky at a dizzying speed, it cast all the colors of the rainbow on the crowd. The crowd began shouting for the Virgin Mary. The strange movements and light from the sun lasted a few minutes before it returned to its natural place in the sky. The crowd, who had been soaked to the skin, was now completely dry. As for the children, they were unaware of any "dance of the sun," they had been communing with Mary.

According to Lucia, "When Our Lady disappeared in the immense distance of the sky, next to the sun we saw Saint Joseph holding the Child Jesus and Our Lady dressed in white with a blue mantle. Saint Joseph seemed to be blessing the world, making the sign of the cross. Shortly after this vision had vanished, I saw Our Lord and Our Lady who reminded me of Our Lady of Sorrows. Our Lord was blessing the world as was Saint Joseph. This vision vanished too, and it seemed to me I again saw Our Lady in a form resembling that of Our Lady of Mount Carmel."

The story of Our Lady of Fatima had worldwide repercussions, and Fatima became a major pilgrimage site. It is visited by five million Marian devotees a year. The three seers were hounded by the sick, the desperate, and the curious. Jacinta and Francisco died during the flu epidemic of 1918. Lucia joined a convent in May 1921. She is still alive at this writing.

Hail Mary, Full of Grace! the Lord is with you; Blessed are you among women, and blessed is the fruit of your womb Jesus. Holy Mary, Mother of God, pray for us sinners, now and at the hour of our death. Amen.

In 1941, Lucia allowed the first two secrets of Fatima to be released. According to her memoir,

> The first part is the vision of hell. Our Lady showed us a great sea of fire which seemed to be under the earth. Plunged in this fire were demons and souls in human form, like transparent burning embers, all blackened or burnished bronze, floating about in the conflagration, now raised into the air by flames that issued from within themselves together with great clouds of smoke, now falling back on every side like sparks in a huge fire, without weight or equilibrium, and amid shrieks and groans of pain and despair, which horrified us and made us tremble with fear. The demons could be distinguished by their terrifying and repulsive likeness to frightful and unknown animals, all black and transparent. This vision lasted but an instant. How can we ever be grateful enough to our kind heavenly mother, who had already prepared us by promising, in the first apparition, to take us to heaven. Otherwise, I think we would have died of fear and terror. We then looked up at Our Lady, who said to us so kindly and sadly, "You have seen hell where the souls of poor sinners go. To save them, God wishes to establish in the world devotion to my Immaculate Heart. If what I say to you is done, many souls will be saved and there will be peace. The war is going to end: but if people do not cease offending God, a worse one will break out during the Pontificate of Pius XI. When you see a night illumined by an unknown light, know that this is the great sign given you by God that he is about to punish the world for its crimes, by means of war, famine and persecutions of the Church. The good will be martyred; the Holy Father will have much to suffer; various nations will be annihilated. In the end, my Immaculate Heart will triumph. The Holy Father will consecrate Russia to me, and she shall be converted, and a period of peace will be granted the world."

Lucia was so confused by the content of the third secret that she placed it in an envelope and sent it to the Vatican with the instructions that it was not to be opened until the year 1960. Pope John XXIII chose not to release it upon reading it, Paul VI also kept it a secret. On May 13, 1981, the Feast of Our Lady of Fatima, an assassin fired a bullet at Pope John Paul II as he was out greeting the pilgrims in Saint Peter's Square. He impulsively bent down to hug a little girl wearing an Our Lady of Fatima medal and the bullet only wounded him instead of killing him. He has always credited Our Lady of Fatima with saving

OUR LADY OF FATIMA IS THE PATRONESS OF PORTUGAL. **The feast day of Our Lady of Fatima is May 13.**

his life. It was he who decided to release the third secret on May 13, 2000, to mark the beatification of Francisco and Jacinta. Lucia met with him beforehand and approved of the action.

This is the third secret as released by the Vatican:

> After the two parts which I have already explained, at the left of Our Lady and a little above, we saw an Angel with a flaming sword in his left hand; flashing, it gave out flames that looked as though they would set the world on fire; but they died out in contact with the splendor that Our Lady radiated towards him from her right hand: pointing to the earth with his right hand, the angel cried out: "Penance, Penance, Penance." And we saw in an immense light that is God: something similar to how people appear in a mirror when they pass in front of it, a bishop dressed in white, we had the impression it was the Holy Father. Other bishops, priests, men and women religious going up a steep mountain, at the top of which there was a big cross of rough-hewn trunks of a cork-tree with the bark; before reaching there the Holy Father passed through a big city half in ruins and trembling with halting step, afflicted with pain and sorrow, he prayed for the souls of the corpses he met on his way. Having reached the top of the mountain, on his knees at the foot of the big cross he was killed by a group of soldiers who fired bullets and arrows at him, and in the same way there died one after another the other bishops, priests, men and women religious, and various laypeople of different ranks and positions. Beneath the two arms of the cross there were two angels each with a crystal aspersorium in their hands, in which they gathered up the blood of the martyrs and with it sprinkled the souls that were making their way to God.

Pope John Paul II felt that this last secret was a symbol of the attempt on his life. The Russian Revolution brought into the world a society that outlawed spirituality and religious practices. By the last half of the twentieth century, communism had engulfed many nations under this umbrella. Coming from Poland, Pope John Paul II was a force to be reckoned with. He inspired many in Russia and Poland to rebel against totalitarian systems. He felt the prayers Our Lady of Fatima asked for and the visions given to the three children helped to change the course of history.

Since it was impossible to walk on the curved dome of the church, the onlookers gathering in the street were astounded to see the woman move onto the dome, bowing and kneeling in front of a cross. It was then that someone yelled out, "It is our Holy Mother Mary!"

Our Lady of Light

The Coptic Church in Egypt celebrates thirty-two feast days in honor of the Virgin Mary. The last one of these falls on April 2 and commemorates Mary under her title of Our Lady of Light. The great majority of Egypt's population is Muslim. The Copts are a Christian sect whose members did not convert when that country was invaded in the eighth century. They make up about 10 percent of Egypt's population. The Copts have a great reverence for the Holy Family since it was to Egypt that Joseph and Mary took the Infant Jesus to hide from Herod. One place where the family rested was Zeitoun near Cairo. When Mary appeared over the Coptic Church of Saint Mark on April 2, 1968, she was seen by a diverse religious crowd. Islamic tradition also has great reverence for Mary. A hadith of the Prophet Muhammad states, "Every child is touched by the devil as soon as he is born and this contact makes him cry. Excepted are Mary and her Son." Like Catholics, the Muslims believe that Mary was a virgin when she conceived Jesus and that she was spiritually superior to all other humans. She is one of eight people who have their own chapter in the Koran. When Mary appeared in Egypt she was welcomed by Coptic Christians, the Protestant Church, the pope's envoy, and the Muslim population.

On April 2, 1968, at 8:30 at night, the mechanics and bus drivers who worked out of the Public Transport Authority heard a disturbance in the street. A young woman dressed in white was on the dome of the Church of Saint Mark across from the garage. Frightened that she was about to kill herself, the Muslim mechanic implored her to be careful, while his compatriot ran to alert the priests. Since it was impossible to walk on the curved dome of the church, the onlookers gathering in the street were astounded to see the woman move onto the dome, bowing and kneeling in front of a cross. It was then that someone yelled out, "It is our Holy Mother Mary!" Cries of "Virgin Mary!" went up from the crowd. As the night sky darkened, the figure of Mary on the roof glowed luminously.

This was the start of a series of hundreds of apparitions that was to last three years. In all of them Mary remained silent but brought a sense of peace and

harmony to the hundreds of thousands in the crowds who would gather to be with her. Not everyone in the crowd saw her, some saw only lights. Others, Muslims as well as Christians viewed her with great clarity. The apparitions became so well-known that they were even broadcast on Egyptian television to an audience of one million people. The Marxist president of Egypt, Abdul Nasser, was among the many political dignitaries who would stand in the street, waiting for Mary. The Egyptian government went so far as to tear down buildings around the church to make room for the ever-expanding crowds.

This silent apparition never appeared at the same time and would come two to three times a week. It was instantly declared a miracle by the Coptic Church when the first man who saw Mary, the mechanic from the garage, went the next day to have a gangrenous finger amputated. Doctors unwrapping his bandages were shocked to find his finger totally healed. Many nights the Virgin would bow to the crowd and bless it; sometimes she appeared with a baby in her arms; many times she waved an olive branch of peace; other times a luminous mist spread everywhere, giving off the scent of incense. A priest at the church has written, "I have seen the Virgin myself reflected against the surface of the moon whose disk got bigger as the moon got nearer to the church. The Virgin made her apparition carrying a babe in her arms." Another witness who watched from his brother's apartment said, "I saw her twice. She was very tall, and she did not stand on the ground. She shone more than the moon, all completely white,

Video clips of the apparitions of the Blessed Virgin Mary made by Egyptian television in Zeitoun, Egypt (1968–1971).

sometimes with her arms together and sometimes with her arms outstretched. Every night there were doves, and doves, you know, do not fly at night." A woman remembering the time of the apparitions said, "There were Muslims and Christians, and everyone was as one, one religion together."

Scientific studies were launched within a fifteen-mile radius of the church. It was thought that the apparition was being projected from somewhere, but no evidence of such an elaborate hoax was ever found. Pope Pius VI's envoy, who witnessed several of the apparitions in the first month, recommended these visions as legitimate visits by Mary. They were widely reported in the newspapers, though not in the West.

OUR LADY OF LIGHT IS THE PATRONESS OF EGYPT.

The feast day of Our Lady of Light is April 2.

Several reasons were suggested for why Mary chose this time and place to appear. One was the disastrous defeat Egypt suffered in the 1967 Six Day War with Israel. Because of it, the Coptic holy sites in Jerusalem were off-limits to Egyptians. Not only was Mary soothing the people in their defeat, she was visiting them when they could not go to the Holy Land to visit her. Another reason was that Zeitoun had sheltered the Holy Family during their flight from Herod, and Mary was revisiting a place that had protected her. The apparitions ended in 1971, when the Egyptian government started to charge admission to stand in the street. There are many black-and-white photographs of these sightings, but original witnesses insist they serve as poor documentation of the luminous visions they remember.

Pray very much the prayers of the rosary. I alone am able to save you from the calamities which approach. Those who place their confidence in me will be saved.

Our Lady of Akita

In previous centuries Marian apparitions were devoted to comforting and encouraging those unfairly suffering. From the apparitions of the Miraculous Medal in the nineteenth century onward, Mary seems more worried and unhappy with the progress of the human race. With the Fatima visits came predictions of another world war if humankind did not reform. At Akita, Japan, toward the end of the twentieth century Mary told a Japanese nun tales of a great chastisement to come if people do not raise themselves up to a more spiritual level. It is felt that the message Mary is delivering in these apparitions is the continuation of those given to the children at Fatima.

Sister Agnes Sasagawa was not yet a Catholic, when at the age of nineteen she was paralyzed because of a medical error while undergoing an appendectomy. Years of painful surgeries and treatments followed, and she became intrigued with the sufferings of Christ and the concept of offering up pain as reparation for others. After converting to Catholicism, she contracted a virus and lapsed into a coma. A priest came to administer the last rites, and eyewitnesses were

quite shocked to hear her reply to him in Latin, a language she had no knowledge of. She remained in the coma for three days and woke up with a beautiful lady standing next to her bed. She prayed the rosary with the lady and after the first decade recited this prayer: "O my Jesus, forgive us our sins/Save us from the fires of hell/Lead all souls to heaven/Especially those in most need of Your mercy."

When a priest heard her recite this prayer, which was unfamiliar to him, he wrote it down. He later told Agnes that this was the prayer the Virgin Mary taught the children at Fatima. It had never been translated into Japanese, and no one in that country had ever heard of it before. After going permanently deaf in 1973, Agnes joined a small convent at Yuzawadi, a remote place on the outskirts of Akita. The mandate of these sisters is to abandon all earthly goods and to lead a life of prayer. On June 12, 1973, while Sister Agnes was praying alone in the chapel, brilliant rays of light began shining from the tabernacle. This overwhelming experience lasted for more than an hour, during which Agnes later said, "Many ideas not of my own making crossed my mind." She was to see this evidence of "divine power" many times after this.

On June 28, 1973, a cross-shaped wound appeared on the inside left hand of Sister Agnes. A week later this wound began to bleed. At three o'clock in the morning on July 6 when Sister Agnes, in great pain, got out of bed to change her bandage, she heard the beautiful lady's voice again telling her to go to the chapel. There she saw a radiant, winged angel who told her, "I am your Guardian Angel. I am assigned to you from all eternity to guide you and care for you." The angel led Sister Agnes to a small wooden statue of Our Lady of Peace that was carved out of a single block of wood by a Buddhist sculptor in 1965. The voice of the lady seemed to be coming from the statue itself, "My daughter, my novice, you have obeyed me well in abandoning all to follow me. Is the infirmity of your ears painful? Your deafness will be healed, be sure. Does the wound of your hand cause you to suffer? Pray in reparation for the sins of men. Each person in this community is my irreplaceable daughter. Do you say well the prayer of the Handmaids of the Eucharist? Then let us pray together." They recited the prayer of their order and by 5:10 a.m. the voice had stopped and the angel had disappeared. The right hand of the statue of the Virgin Mary was bleeding.

OUR LADY OF AKITA IS THE PATRONESS OF JAPAN.

On August 3, 1973, Sister Agnes experienced the second message from the statue.

"If you love the Lord, listen to what I have to say to you. It is very important; you will convey it to your superior. Many men in this world afflict the Lord. I desire souls to console him to soften the anger of the heavenly Father. I wish, with my Son, for souls who will repair by their suffering and their poverty for the sinners and ingrates. In order that the world might know his anger, the heavenly Father is preparing to inflict a great chastisement on all mankind. I have intervened so many times to appease the wrath of the Father. . . . Prayer, penance and courageous sacrifices can soften the Father's anger. . . . Even in a secular institute, prayer is necessary. Already souls who wish to pray are on the way to being gathered together. Without attaching too much attention to the form, be faithful and fervent in prayer to console the Master."

The wound in the statue's hand disappeared on September 29, 1973. The nuns noticed that, while the blood had stopped flowing from the statue, it now seemed to be "sweating," its head and neck covered in moisture.

On October 13, 1973, the anniversary of the last apparition of Our Lady of Fatima, the voice in the statue spoke again, telling Sister Agnes that this was the last message she would hear.

"Listen carefully to what I say to you and inform your superior. If humanity does not repent and improve, the Eternal Father will allow a terrible punishment to befall all humankind. This punishment will be worse than the flood or any that has ever been seen before. A fire will fall from the sky and annihilate large numbers. Neither priests nor the faithful will be spared. The survivors will be in such desolation they will envy the dead. The only weapons that will remain will be the rosary and the sign that the Eternal Father will leave. Pray the rosary every day. The work of the devil will infiltrate even into the Church in such a way that one will see Cardinals opposing Cardinals, Bishops against other Bishops. The priests who venerate me will scorned and opposed by their confreres. Churches and altars will be sacked. The Church will be full of those who accept compromises and the demon will press many priests and consecrated souls to leave the service of the Lord. The demon will be especially implacable against the souls consecrated to God. The thought of the loss of so many souls is the cause of my sadness. If sins increase in number and gravity, there will be no longer pardon for them. . . . Pray very much the prayers of the rosary. I alone am able to save you from the calamities which approach. Those who place their confidence in me will be saved."

From January 4, 1975, until September 15, 1981 (the Feast of Our Lady of Sorrows), the statue in the chapel wept 101 times. This was witnessed by the town officials, psychologists, medical doctors, and members of the clergy. Five hundred witnesses, Christian and Buddhist, signed testimony that they have seen this statue shed blood, sweat, and tears. Because Sister Agnes regained her hearing as promised and a Korean woman was cured of an inoperable brain tumor, the local church officials took the apparitions seriously. After years of study and testimony they accepted this visit of Mary as a true apparition. The Vatican has partially approved it. In recognizing this apparition, Bishop Ito of Japan has written that it is difficult to believe an apparition where Our Lady has delivered such a terrible message. But in her message she also points out that the chastisement she speaks of is on the condition "if men don't better themselves." It is also true that fire from the sky is not just a nightmarish "what if" scenario for the Japanese people. It is a historical fact. The atomic bomb that was dropped on Nagasaki in August 1945 had at its ground zero Urakami Cathedral. At that time Nagasaki was the center of Japanese Catholicism. Ironically, that one atomic attack killed more Japanese Christians than hundreds of years of official persecution.

When the people saw this lighter-skinned version of Our Lady of the Hermits they refused to accept it. "It is not ours," they said. "Ours used to be black."

Black Madonnas

Wherever Mary appears in the world, she ethnically resembles the people who see her. Standard art images of Mary are those that have been created by western European artists, and the white European version of Mary is the one that is most common around the world. Few people realize that the oldest art images of Mary and Jesus portray them as dark brown or black. In Europe alone there are at least five hundred Black Madonnas. They all have large groups of white European devotees. France, Spain, Germany, Switzerland, Poland, the Canary Islands, and Italy have very popular pilgrimage sites connected with their Black Madonnas. With the exception of the Polish icon Our Lady of Czestochowa, these Black Madonnas are all statues. Most legends around them say that they were carved by Saint Luke, as direct portraits of the Virgin Mary while she was alive. Many have been found in caves or washed up on the shore. In Zaragoza, Spain, the Virgin Mary herself gave the statue known as the Virgen del Pilar, Our Lady of Pilar, to Saint James as an act of encouragement for his mission there. The Holy House of Loreto, purported to be the Virgin's own house, has a very famous Black Madonna. Chartres Cathedral, considered in itself the most magnificent shrine to Mary, displays the Vierge Noire de Notre Dame de Pilier in a prominent place near the main altar. Tourists have often commented on the stream of devotees whom they witness visiting her. Le Puy, in France, is considered the first place the Virgin Mary appeared after her Assumption into heaven. Their Black Madonna and the people's fervid devotion to her so threatened the leaders of the French Revolution that they had it taken to Paris, publicly mocked, guillotined,

N. D. de Loreto

SUISSE

and burned. This did not stop the residents of Le Puy from creating a replica of the original statue and honoring it with the same enthusiasm.

The Russian and Eastern Orthodox Churches have many icons with a dark brown Mary and Jesus. Many of them were sent to the West to avoid destruction at the hands of Iconoclasts. The region where southern France meets northern Spain is especially rich in local shrines. Because Mary Magdalen is said to have traveled to and died as a hermit in this region, it is common to find shrines to her in the same area as the Black Madonnas. This gave rise to the theory that the Black Madonna is not the Virgin Mary and Jesus but actually Mary Magdalen and the son she allegedly had with Jesus. This theory takes things a step further by saying that devotees of the Black Madonnas make up a hidden society which knows the secret of Jesus's bloodline. Intriguing as this idea is, it does not explain why Italy, which has no special devotion to Mary Magdalen would have the greatest number of Black Madonnas.

The common official explanation given for these dark-skinned Marys is that they have been blackened by the constant and ever-present smoke from candles or that they have been carved from wood that has darkened over the centuries. Yet, when reading about Mary statues that have undergone restoration and have been cleaned up and lightened, the devotees always insist that their Mary should remain permanently black. That is how the people know her and feel most comfortable with her.

Another popular theory put forth is the one of the Black Madonnas' connection to ancient goddesses who were worshiped by the local populace. While the Roman Empire flourished the cult of Isis was widespread. The statue of Isis holding her son Horus on her lap was always carved out of black basalt. Like Mary, Isis was considered a holy virgin who gave birth. The Mediterranean region and Gaul were major centers for Isis worshipers. In southern Italy another black goddess reigned, Cybele, the goddess of fertility and the earth. Her places of worship were always in caves situated in a

First Communion procession, Hoboken, New Jersey, circa 1950.

spectacular setting. Many of the Black Madonnas were supposedly found in caves in craggy aeries high above surrounding land. Artemis of Ephesus, another fertility goddess, was also very popular in these regions. She, too, was portrayed only in black stone. According to some theories, in order to convert the pagan populations to Christianity, early evangelists simply renamed popular goddesses and absorbed their cults into the Church.

A simpler idea has been put forth that the real color of Mary and Jesus was brown. Since there are no physical descriptions of them in the scriptures and they did hail from the Middle East, it is highly probable that their skin color was actually dark brown and these ancient portraits are based on handed-down descriptions from original eyewitness accounts. There is a painting of a Black Mary and Jesus over the portal of the Church of the Nativity in Bethlehem, alleged to be Jesus's birthplace. When a priest in Lucera, Italy, was questioned by a visitor on why his church's Madonna was black, he had a simple answer, "My son, she is black because she is black."

Many small towns have their own Black Madonna, and miraculous healings are a major part of their attraction. These dark-skinned Marys have a strong sense of mystery, and devotion to them is especially deep and profound. Their stories of being found in caves or washed up on shore by the waves show Mary in a more humble light—as someone who need not live in a palace but whose kingdom is the very earth she surrounds herself with. The Black Madonnas are more than just an inclusion of all humanity in Mary, they also bring back the ancient devotion to earth as the Great Mother.

Our Lady of Czestochowa

Our Lady of Czestochowa is the most well-known and most revered of the many Black Madonna icons found in the East. Not only is this image honored in the traditional way as an icon, but, like Our Lady of Guadalupe, Our Lady of Czestochowa has earned the dedication of an entire nation. She has been credited several times with saving Poland from invaders and providing a national identity when the country was divided. The Polish people not only admire her as an aspect of the Virgin Mary, but they also relate to her as their queen and credit their existence as a nation to her help.

Like the majority of the Black Madonna statues, it is said that Our Lady of Czestochowa was created by Saint Luke. The historical legend of this painting is that the Virgin Mary actually sat for it after the Crucifixion when she was living in the house of Saint John the Evangelist. The cedar wood the icon was painted on was from a table made by Jesus Christ when he was a carpenter. During the destruction of Jerusalem in A.D. 70, the early Christians hid the painting away. It was rediscovered in A.D. 326 when Saint Helena, the elderly mother of Constantine made her trip to the Holy Land in her search for the True Cross. Among the relics she brought back with her to Constantinople was this icon. Constantine erected a church to house the image, and it was revered by the citizens of that city. The icon remained in Constantinople for five centuries, escaping destruction during the reign of the Iconoclasts (746–843). This was a movement in the Eastern Church that strictly forbade the existence of religious images. All icons and holy pictures were ordered painted over or destroyed. It is said that the wife of the emperor who ordered it burned hid the icon away instead. In the ninth century Constantinople's emperor offered Charlemagne any

treasure he wanted in the city in gratitude for his help in defending them against the Saracen invaders. Charlemagne chose this icon and later presented it to Prince Leo of Ruthenia. It remained in his castle at Belz, Russia, for the next five hundred years. In 1349, an invasion mounted by the Tartars from the east threatened Belz. Prince Ladislaus, the town's ruler, decided to take the icon to a safer place. As he was making his plans, an arrow fired by the invaders came through the window and embedded itself in the painting. It was the prince's intention to take the painting to his birthplace in Opala. While he stopped to rest in the town called Czestochowa, the image was brought to Jasna Gora ("bright hill") and temporarily placed in the Church of the Assumption. On August 26, 1382, when the prince attempted to continue his journey, the painting became too heavy for his servants to carry. He took this as a sign from the Virgin Mary that this painting should remain in Czestochowa. Searching for the holiest men he could find to create a shrine, he brought in an order of Hungarian monks dedicated to Saint Paul the Hermit to guard the icon. This is also where the first writings on the painting start to be recorded.

The followers of a heretic priest John Hus of Prague stormed the church in 1430. In an attempt to rob the jewels embedded in the icon, one of the men started slashing at the icon's face. As he was about to slash it a third time, he fell dead. This terrified the invaders into leaving. The icon, however, fell and broke into three pieces. Grecian painters familiar with the style of iconic painting were brought in to restore it, and by 1434 it was virtually completely repainted. However, the two slashes in the face have continually reappeared despite repeated attempts to repair them.

OUR LADY OF CZESTOCHOWA IS THE PATRONESS OF POLAND. **Her feast day is August 26.**

In 1655 a small army of three hundred Polish soldiers were gathered at the foot of the monastery. They were challenged by a force of twelve thousand Swedish invaders. In one of the greatest victories in European history, the small army of Poles successfully routed the invasion. Though the image of Our Lady of Czestochowa had always been regarded as special and miraculous, this victory was considered spectacular proof of the intercession of Mary through the icon. On April 1, 1656, King John Casimir proclaimed Our Lady of Czestochowa as Queen of Poland, and said vows putting the country under her patronage and protection. On September 3, 1717, the apostolic delegate staged a national coronation of the icon. A crown, given to Poland as a gift from the pope, was created to fit on the head in the image. In the late eighteenth century, Poland had a very weak central government and it was gradually separated and divided up by Russia, Austria, and Prussia. Throughout this time, under foreign domination, almost every Polish church had a copy of Our Lady of Czestochowa and the people consistently referred to her as the Queen of Poland. Until the country's restoration in 1918, the shrine at Jasna Gora served as a spiritual capital and a vital link for the Polish people with their true homeland.

In the last century, on September 14, 1920, the Russian army was gathered at the Vistula River in preparation for an invasion of Warsaw. The Polish people prayed to Our Lady of Czestochowa for a miracle. The Russians dispersed the next day when they saw the image of the Virgin Mary in the clouds over Warsaw. In Polish history books this is known as the Miracle of Vistula.

The Pauline Fathers at Jasna Gora keep archives of all the individual claims of healings and miracles due to the intercession of Our Lady of Czestochowa. National devotion to her remains very strong, and her shrine has been a popular pilgrimage site since her arrival in the late fourteenth century. As the people of that country suffered through division and annexation, the Nazi invasion and Communist rule, they have always remained steadfast in keeping her feast day.

Many people are puzzled as to why Our Lady of Czestochowa is dark-skinned. Different explanations are given: the ancient paints have darkened over time, or it was made darker when it was overpainted in the fifteenth century, or that centuries of candle smoke have blackened the image. It is also commonly said that when the original shrine at Jasna Gora was destroyed by fire, though the painting, miraculously, did not burn, it was darkened by the flames and smoke and from that day on it has been known as the Black Madonna.

In the early part of the twentieth century the original crown for the icon was taken by thieves, but an elaborate new crown was created to replace it. In some images, Our Lady of Czestochowa wears this elaborate crown and in others, she wears the royal blue veil of the Virgin Mary.

Our Lady of Pilar—the Virgen del Pilar

Zaragoza, in northeastern Spain, has been a sacred site since prehistory. Many pilgrims visiting it insist that it exudes a magnetic charge that is rarely found in the Western world. The ancient Celts called this settlement on the Ebro River, Salduba. When they were conquered by the Romans in the early part of the first century B.C., the name was changed to Caesraugusta after the Roman emperor. It was to this region that the apostle James the Greater came to evangelize about the recently risen Christ. After much labor, James was able to convert only eight disciples. Distraught over the presumed failure of his mission, he went to pray along the banks of the Ebro River. Deep in his meditation he heard celestial singing; when he looked up he saw the Virgin Mary standing on a pillar. She smilingly told him that she had come to help him, and she asked James to build a chapel there, promising to "remain at the site until the end of time, so that the grace of God will work omens and marvels through my intercession for those who, in their hour of need, invoked my name." She then disappeared, leaving behind the pillar with a little wood statue of herself holding the Christ Child.

Legend has it that this visitation took place in A.D. 40, at the time the Virgin Mary was still alive. It is explained that she was either transported to Spain by angels or she bilocated, a gift common among mystical saints who are able to be in two places at once. Greatly energized and encouraged by this visit, James and his eight followers, who all saw the apparition, worked together on building the first church in western Europe, dedicating it to Santa Maria del Pilar (Holy Mary of the Pillar). The little chapel that was constructed became a regional center for the conversion of pagans.

For the past two thousand years many wars and invaders have tried to conquer this valuable territory, and the little chapel housing the statue has been destroyed over and over again. The people of the region made sure that no one was ever able to desecrate or destroy the statue. A large basilica, dedicated to housing the statue, was consecrated in 1686. A visit to see this statue is an important stop on the trail to Santiago de Compostela, the burial place of Saint James.

It is said in Zaragosa that the church of the Virgen del Pilar was the first dedicated in Mary's honor and that it will last as long as the faith.

The Madonna del Tindari

Tindari is a small city in the province of Messina, Sicily. It has ancient roots as a Greek colony centuries before Christ. From prehistoric times the local people have honored the goddess Cybele whose cult dates back to about 6000 B.C. In Asia Minor she was known as the Great Mother, a Mother Earth figure who ruled over fertility. Her places of worship were typically caves set on rocky cliffs. The pre-Classic Greeks referred to her as "Mother of the Gods, the Savior

THE MADONNA DEL TINDARI IS THE PATRONESS OF TINDARI, SICILY. **Her feast day is the Birthday of Mary, September 8.**

Our Lady of Pilar is sometimes depicted as white.
The original wooden statue is known as the first of the Black Madonnas.

who hears our prayers" or "the Mother of the Gods, the Accessible One." In art, the standard image of Cybele is of her seated on a throne, her hand resting on the neck of a serene lion and the other holding a tambourine-shaped instrument reminiscent of the full moon.

According to legend, the Black Madonna statue of Tindari was brought to that shore by sailors who had hidden the statue from the iconoclastic destruction then raging in the East. When a storm forced them to land at Tindari, they entrusted the statue to a group of monks who had settled on the cliffs. Another version of the story is similar to Our Lady of Montserrat, where shepherds found the little statue of the "Madonna Bruna" (Dark Madonna) in a cave on Tindari. A note in Latin on parchment was with her, which reads "I am black but beautiful, O you daughters of Jerusalem" (Song of Solomon 1:5).

The people of that region are extremely devoted to this brown Madonna enthroned with her Son. Wherever they have emigrated to in the world, they bring her festival celebrating the Madonna del Tindari.

Our Lady of Montserrat

About twenty miles from Barcelona and four thousand feet above sea level is the Shrine of Our Lady of Montserrat. Affectionately known as "La Morenata" (The Dark Maiden), this thirtyeight-inch-tall Black Madonna has been the subject of veneration for well over a thousand years. According to legend, this wooden statue of Mary and the Christ Child was carved by Saint Luke and brought to Spain by Saint Peter in A.D. 50. During the Moorish invasions of the eighth century, it was thought that the statue was taken away and hidden in a cave at Montserrat to save it from destruction. The mountain itself is made up of craggy perpendicular boulders and was virtually inaccessible to outsiders. In the year 890, a group of shepherds tending their flocks saw strange lights and heard singing coming from the mountain. Too frightened to investigate this

OUR LADY OF MONTSERRAT IS THE PATRONESS OF CATALONIA.

The feast day of Our Lady of Montserrat is the same as for Our Lady of Refuge, January 16.

127

supernatural event, they brought the bishop of Manresa to the cave. Upon entering, he found a wood figure of Mary and the Holy Child holding the globe of the world in his hand. A church was built high on the rocks near where the statue was found.

Written records of the arrival of this statue go back to 932. The royalty of Barcelona put the shrine and the protection of the Madonna under their patronage. Because of the difficulty in reaching the church, it has always been a pilgrimage place for the most devout. When Saint Ignatius Loyola was a soldier, he spent a night meditating and praying in front of the statue before he totally changed his life path. Spain's greatest saints have all spent time at Montserrat.

There is a story that the mountain was once a smooth boulder. At the time of the Crucifixion of Jesus, when the sun darkened, there was a massive earthquake in Montserrat. When light returned, the mountain had a thousand peaks. Montserrat is the Latin word for "saw-edged mountain." Because of its mysterious and fantastic placement, it has always been mentioned as one of the former sanctuaries of the Holy Grail.

The statue itself carbon-dates back to the twelfth century. Its style is obviously Romanesque. The enthroned Virgin is very typical of how Mary was portrayed in those times. A theory has been offered that perhaps the statue the shepherds found was really a version of Isis and Horus. Catalonia had been a Roman settlement in the early first century A.D. and the cult of Isis had flourished there. Since Isis was always carved in black basalt, when this replacement statue was created, it, too, was made black, though modeled on the Christian iconography of the Enthroned Virgin.

OUR LADY OF EINSIEDELN IS THE PATRONESS OF SWITZERLAND. **The feast day of Our Lady of Einsiedeln is September 14.**

Our Lady of Einsiedeln

The statue of Our Lady of Einsiedeln is said to be material proof of the power of prayer and the ability of meditation to change the vibrations and feelings of a place hundreds of years into the future. Brother Meinrad, a Benedictine monk, left his monastery at Richenau in 840 in order to move into the woods and live as a hermit. It was firmly believed that anchorites and hermits served the world by being in a state of constant prayer. At first Meinrad lived in a cave near his monastery. But as it was the custom in ancient times to look upon hermits as those with great wisdom, too many of the local people came to him for advice. He moved to a much more isolated place where there were no human settlements. He erected his hermitage with a chapel, his cell, and two small rooms to shelter travelers. His belongings were a candlestick, a missal, a Bible, a copy of the Rule of Saint Benedict, and a statue of Mary holding the Christ Child. This statue had been given to him by Hildegard, the abbess of Zurich. Meinrad was devoted to the Virgin Mary, and he lived in this isolated environment for twenty years, conversing with the trees, the flowers, and the animals. The people of the valley respected his privacy and admired his sanctity. In 863, two robbers who suspected that Meinrad was secretly hiding a great treasure went to the hermitage asking for shelter. After Meinrad took them in, they killed him with the candlestick. Being at one with nature, it is said that Meinrad had two crows as his guardians. The two robbers were not only angry and disappointed at not finding any treasure, but they were also terrified by the two crows who flew around their heads, pursuing them all the way back to Zurich. The crows did not leave them until they were identified as the murderers of the holy man.

Meinrad's cell quickly became a place where people went for spiritual favors and healing. So great was Meinrad's devotion to Mary, that the people felt she had a special love for those who visited the place he spent in prayer. His cell became known as the Lady Chapel, and soon a community of hermits came to live in the same place. In 940 a new Benedictine monastery was erected, which enclosed the cell of Meinrad. Today, it is the abbey of Einsiedeln, Switzerland.

In 948 a church was built around the Lady Chapel of Einsiedeln. On September 14, the day before the consecration ceremony, the church was filled with a blinding light and the bishop saw a vision of Jesus Christ on the altar. When he went the next day to perform the Consecration, he heard a voice clearly tell him that the church had already been consecrated to God. His deposition is still intact and preserved at the abbey. Meinrad's statue, called Our Lady of the Hermits continued to be the focal point for pilgrims. After almost one thousand years of a peaceful existence, in the spring of 1798, the sanctuary was invaded by French revolutionary troops. They sent what they thought was Meinrad's statue back to Paris and razed the Lady Chapel. In reality, the people of Einsiedeln hid the statue. It was deemed safe to return it to the church in 1802 but first it was restored in Austria. The restorer took great care in removing centuries of smoke grime from the statue. When the people saw this lighter-skinned version of Our Lady of the Hermits they refused to accept it. "It is not ours," they said. "Ours used to be black." He had to blacken the skin of the statue in order to make it acceptable to them.

It is believed that the statue that is at present displayed in the chapel is not Meinrad's original but a copy that was made in 1466 after a fire had struck the church. It is important to note that grace abounds in the place that Meinrad spent his days in prayer devoted to the Virgin Mary. He successfully created a peaceful atmosphere in that place, regardless of the fact that his original hermitage and original statue no longer exist.

By concentrating on these terrible sorrows it becomes apparent how much human suffering there is in the world. But every one of these sad events is erased with the act of Christ's Resurrection.

Our Lady of Sorrows

One of the reasons that the Virgin Mary is held in such awe by Catholics is that she suffered so much over the fate of her Son, and yet even as she faced His agonizing death on Cavalry, she never looked away, she accepted His fate with great faith. She knew His future when He was a child, yet she let Him go to live it out. She did not try to dissuade Him or hide Him away. No matter what suffering we go through, we know Mary can empathize with us. She was poor, she suffered the gossip of others by being pregnant and unmarried, her family was homeless, and her Son was unfairly condemned, imprisoned, and executed.

By concentrating on the Seven Sorrows of Mary, those in deep despair can eventually realize that all sadness, fear, and dread will end by the grace-filled example Mary set. After Christ's Resurrection, Mary has turned her attention to humanity. In several of her apparitions she is crying and tearful. She is again the Sorrowful Mother, this time crying for all of her children.

Uitgave van Canisiusblad.

Ook door uwe eigene ziel zal een zweerd gaan. (Luc. II. 35.)

S⁺ Augustinus' drukkerij,

In art, Our Lady of Sorrows is the Mater Dolorosa, a woman in tears. Often her heart is exposed with seven swords in it, and she holds the crown of thorns from the Passion.

The Seven Sorrows of Mary are the following:

1] The Prophecy of Simeon. When Joseph and Mary presented Jesus in the Temple, the holy man Simeon, who had been touched by the Holy Spirit, predicted everything that was to happen to him. "Behold, this child is destined for the fall and rise of many in Israel, and to be a sign that will be contradicted (and you yourself a sword will pierce) so that thoughts of many hearts may be revealed" (Luke 2:34–35). This is where the pictorial concept of showing Mary with a pierced heart comes from.

BEATA VERGINE ADDOLORATA

The Mother of sorrows. Madre dolorosa.
La Madre di dolore. A Mãe dolorosa.
DIE MUTTER DER SCHMERZEN

L. BOUASSE Jne Édr   702   RUE MABILLON, 9, PARIS

Nossa Senhora das Dôres.

Nᵗ⁰ Sᵗᵃ DE LOS DOLORES + Mᵗⁱᵃ Sᵗⁱᵃ ADDOLORATA.
Our Lady of Dolours.

PL. 306.

132

2] The Flight into Egypt. After the departure of the Wise Men, an angel appeared to Joseph in his sleep and told him of Herod's plans to slaughter all the male children in Bethlehem under the age of two in order to prevent the coming of Christ. Jesus and Mary, in fear for their Son's safety, had to sneak out of Bethlehem in the dead of night and take an untraveled and secretive route to Egypt. There they remained until Herod's death.

The feast day of Our Lady of Sorrows is September 15.

3] The Loss of the Child Jesus in the Temple. Every Passover the Holy Family and their relatives traveled by caravan to Jerusalem. After the feast was over, they would all travel home. When Jesus was twelve years old, and the extended family was returning to Galilee, Joseph and Mary assumed Jesus was with other family members. When they began looking for him, no one knew where he was. They rushed back to Jerusalem to search for him and did not find him until the third day. He was sitting in the Temple courts lecturing to the teachers there. Mary, who was astonished, said, "Son, why have you treated us like this? Your father and I have been anxiously searching for you." Jesus calmly replied, "Why were you searching for me? Didn't you know I had to be in my Father's house?" (Luke 2:41–51). This was Mary's first realization that Jesus was no mortal child and that in the future He would do things that she had no control over.

4] The Meeting of Jesus and Mary on the Way of the Cross. Mary was in the crowd watching every insult and violent act perpetrated against her Son. As he struggled and fell, the crowd laughed at him. She, as His mother, could do nothing.

5] The Crucifixion. All of Jesus's disciples except for John and Mary Magdelen ran away from him as he was nailed to the Cross. His mother never flinched or deserted him. She never left the foot of His Cross throughout His agony while He slowly died.

6] The Taking Down of the Body of Jesus from the Cross. Mary held her dead Son covered in wounds. The visual image in painting and sculpture of this, her greatest sorrow, is known as the "Pietà."

7] The Burial of Jesus. When they rolled the stone across Christ's tomb Mary must have lost hope that she would ever see Him again. Her faith must have wavered, and she must have felt that all the good her Son had done for others was in vain.

By concentrating on these terrible sorrows it becomes apparent how much human suffering there is in the world. But every one of these sad events is erased with the act of Christ's Resurrection. In this way, Our Lady of Sorrows prepares us to conquer all worldly pain.

In the early thirteenth century Saint Dominic had a vision of the Virgin Mary where she handed him a Rosary and made fifteen promises to those who said it on a daily basis.

In many of her apparitions, particularly those of the twentieth century, the Virgin Mary has implored all of humanity to say the Rosary in order to change the hearts of humankind. Why the insistence on this repetitive prayer?

The world's most ancient religions have used repetitive prayer to raise followers' mental states to a more mystical plane. The practice of counting prayers with stones goes back thousands of years before Christ. The earliest Christian monks retired from the world repeating a simple prayer over and over, "Lord Jesus Christ, Son of God, have mercy upon me." Medieval monks reported entering an altered state where they saw a powerful light around them after repeating this prayer for hours in a day. Even if one has no feeling for the words in the prayer, it is a starting point to empty the clutter of the material world out of the mind. Scientific research on individuals who habitually chant mantras or repeat prayers documented that these subjects had lower stress levels, higher immune systems, less frequent insomnia, and lower blood pressure than the average population. They also had a calmer reaction to stressful situations and were much less apt to react in a violent or paranoid manner.

Medieval people loved Mary. The Hail Mary was developed from the

scriptural greetings of the angel Gabriel in Luke's Gospel. Like the Our Father, this was a simple prayer, easy for the uneducated laity to remember. Repeating these prayers several times brought one into a heightened state of grace. Eventually, the monks taught the great events of Jesus Christ's life through the Rosary by developing a ritualistic, formulaic series of prayers that was accessible to the masses. The method of using prayer beads to count one's prayers goes back to the earliest monks. The Rosary, a series of fifty beads divided up into tens separated by an individual one, has evolved from the Middle Ages. The directions for saying the Rosary are very simple: for each bead in the decade one says a Hail Mary, for each separating bead an Our Father is said. On each decade while one is repeating the rote prayer, a scriptural event in the life of Christ is meditated on. On one day the Joyful Mysteries are considered, on another the Sorrowful Mysteries and on another the Glorious Mysteries.

The Joyful Mysteries: The Annunciation (Luke 1:30–33), The Visitation (Luke 1:50–53), The Nativity (Luke 2:10–11), The Presentation (Luke 2:29–32), The Finding in the Temple (Luke 2:48–52).

The Sorrowful Mysteries: The Agony in the Garden (Matthew 26:38–39), The Scourging at the Pillar (John 19:1), The Crowning with Thorns (Mark 15:16–17), The Carrying of the Cross (John 19:17), The Crucifixion (John 19: 28–30).

The Glorious Mysteries: The Resurrection (Mark 16:6–8), The Ascension (Acts 1:10–11), The Coming of the Holy Spirit (Acts 2:1–4), The Assumption of Mary (Song of Songs 2:3–6), The Coronation of Mary (Luke 1:51–54).

Saying five decades of the Rosary takes approximately fifteen to twenty minutes each day. The beads tend to regulate the amount of time one spends concentrating on each mystery. When Mary requests the world to say the Rosary, she is asking us to review the story of Christ's life. The act of saying the Rosary is one that pulls the mind out of the material world and brings on a state of calm. Violent feelings and blind hatreds dissipate. The recitation of rote prayers is just a starting point in entering a more spiritual level of thought.

In the early thirteenth century Saint Dominic had a vision of the Virgin Mary where she handed him a Rosary and made fifteen promises to those who said it on a daily basis:

1] Whoever shall faithfully serve me by the recitation of the Rosary, shall receive signal graces.

2] I promise my special protection and the greatest graces to all those who shall recite the Rosary.

3] The Rosary shall be a powerful armor against hell, it will destroy vice, decrease sin, and defeat heresies.

4] It will cause virtue and good works to flourish; it will obtain for souls the abundant mercy of God; it will withdraw the hearts of people from the love of the world and its vanities, and will lift them to the desire of eternal things. O, that souls would sanctify themselves by this means.

5] The soul which recommends itself to me by the recitation of the Rosary, shall not perish.

6] Whoever shall recite the Rosary devoutly, applying themselves to the consideration of its Sacred Mysteries, shall never be conquered by misfortune. God will not chastise them in His justice, they shall not perish by an unprovided death; if they be just, they shall remain in the grace of God, and become worthy of eternal life.

THE ROSARY IS A UNIVERSAL DEVOTION.

The Feast of Our Lady of the Rosary is October 7.

7] Whoever shall have a true devotion for the Rosary shall not die without the Sacraments of the Church.

8] Those who are faithful to recite the Rosary shall have during their life and at their death the light of God and the plentitude of His graces; at the moment of death they shall participate in the merits of the Saints in Paradise.

9] I shall deliver from purgatory those who have been devoted to the Rosary.

10] The faithful children of the Rosary shall merit a high degree of glory in Heaven.

11] You shall obtain all you ask of me by the recitation of the Rosary.

12] All those who propagate the Holy Rosary shall be aided by me in their necessities.

13] I have obtained from my divine Son that all the advocates of the Rosary shall have for intercessors the entire celestial court during their life and the hour of death.

14] All who recite the Rosary are my children, and brothers and sisters of my only Son, Jesus Christ.

15] Devotion of my Rosary is a great sign of predestination.

Hail Mary Full of Grace! the Lord is with you; Blessed are you among women, and blessed is the fruit of your womb Jesus. Holy Mary, Mother of God, pray for us sinners, now and at the hour of our death. Amen.

Feast Days of Mary

January 1 ✣ Mary, Mother of God
January 21 ✣ Our Lady of Altagracia
January 23 ✣ Espousal of the Virgin Mary
January 24 ✣ Madonna del Pianto (Our Lady of Tears)

February 2 ✣ Purification of Mary
February 11 ✣ Our Lady of Lourdes

March 25 ✣ The Annuciation

April 25 ✣ Our Lady of Good Counsel (at Genazzano)
April 26 ✣ Our Lady of Good Counsel (elsewhere)

May 13 ✣ Our Lady of Fatima
May 13 ✣ Our Lady of the Most Blessed Sacrament
May 24 ✣ Mary, Help of Christians
May 31 ✣ Mary, Mediatrix of All Graces
May 31 ✣ The Visitation

June 9 ✣ Mary, Virgin Mother of Grace
June 27 ✣ Our Lady of Perpetual Help

July 2 ✣ Visitation by Mary to Saint Elizabeth
July 16 ✣ Our Lady of Mount Carmel
July 17 ✣ Humility of the Blessed Virgin Mary

August 2 ✣ Our Lady of the Angels
August 5 ✣ Our Lady of the Snow
August 5 ✣ Our Lady of the Copacabana
August 13 ✣ Our Lady, Refuge of Sinners

August 15 ✣ The Assumption into Heaven
August 21 ✣ Our Lady of Knock
August 22 ✣ Immaculate Heart of Mary
August 22 ✣ Queenship of Mary

September 8 ✣ Nativity of Mary
September 8 ✣ Our Lady of Charity
September 12 ✣ Most Holy Name Mary
September 15 ✣ Our Lady of Sorrow
September 24 ✣ Our Lady of Mercy
September 24 ✣ Our Lady of Walsingham

October 1 ✣ Holy Protection of the Mother of God
October 7 ✣ Our Lady of the Most Holy Rosary
October 11 ✣ Maternity of the Blessed Virgin Mary
October 16 ✣ Maternity of the Blessed Virgin Mary

November 21 ✣ Presentation of Mary at the Temple

December 8 ✣ The Immaculate Conception
December 12 ✣ Our Lady of Guadalupe
December 18 ✣ Expectation of the Blessed Virgin Mary

Moveable Feasts:

Saturday after Ascension ✣ Our Lady, Queen
of the Apostles

Saturday before the last Sunday in August ✣
Our Lady, Health of the Sick

Saturday after the Feast of Saint Augustine (August 28) ✣
Our Lady of Consolation

Saturday before third Sunday of November ✣
Mary, Mother of Divine Providence

FOLLOWING PAGES: Procession in honor of
The Blessed Virgin Mary in Sicily, Italy.

Bibliography

Connell, Janice T. *Meetings with Mary: Visions of the Blessed Mother.*
New York: Ballantine Books, 1995.

Durham, Michael S. *Miracles of Mary: Apparitions, Legends, and Miraculous Works of the Blessed Virgin Mary.*
California: HarperSanFrancisco, 1995.

Harris, Ruth. *Lourdes: Body and Spirit in the Secular Age.*
New York: Penguin Books, 1996.

Johnson, Kevin O. *Rosary Mysteries, Meditations, and the Telling of the Beads.*
New York: Pangaeus Press, 1996.

United States Catholic Church. *The Catechism of the Catholic Church.*
New York: Doubleday, 1995.

Websites:

The Catholic Encyclopedia
www.newadvent.org

Carmelite Website
www.carmelite.org

The Mary Page
The Marian Library/International Marian Research Institute at the University of Dayton in Ohio
www.udayton.edu/mary/main.html

Official Website of the Vatican
www.vatican.va

The Church of Our Lady of Zeitoun
www.zeitun-eg.org

Picture Credits

All holy cards are from the collection of Micki Cesario, except for those on pages 18 top left, bottom left, top right, 19, bottom right, 22, top left, bottom right, 69, 81,117 and 132 bottom right, which are from the collection of Father Eugene Carrella and on pages 25 and 118 which are from the collection of Joseph Sciorra.

Other pictures are from the following sources:

Courtesy of the Church of Our Lady of Zeitoun in Egypt: p. 110.

The Marian Library at the University of Dayton in Ohio: pp. 119, 127.

Courtesy of the New York Public Library: p. 140.

E. Quinault, courtesy of the Museum of New Mexico: p. 72.

Larry Racioppo: pp. 10, 26, 44, 58–59, 74, 84, 90.

Dana Salvo: pp. 91–92.

Joseph Sciorra, courtesy of the Societá di Mutuo Soccorso Santa Febronia Patti e Circondario, Hoboken, New Jersey: p. 118.

Courtesy of the Shrine of Our Lady of Akita in Japan: p. 113.

Lisa Silvestri: pp., 2, 6, 13–14, 28, 30, 35–36, 38–39, 41, 50, 53, 56, 61, 86–88, 94, 95, 137.